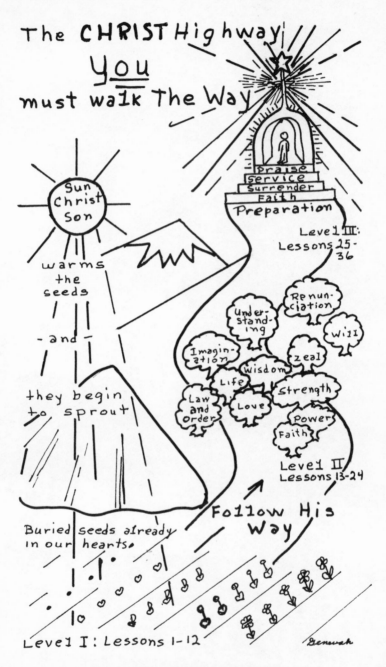

The CHRIST Highway

YOU must walk The Way

Sun Christ Son

warms the seeds

- and -

they begin to sprout

Buried seeds already in our hearts.

Level I: Lessons 1-12

Praise
Service
Surrender
Faith
Preparation

Level III: Lessons 25-36

Renunciation

Understanding

Will

Imagination

Zeal

Wisdom

Life

Law and Order

Love

Strength

Power

Faith

Level II Lessons 13-24

Follow His Way

Genevah

"And a Highway shall be there and a Way,
and it shall be called the 'Way of Holiness.'"

(Isaiah 35:8)

THE CHRIST HIGHWAY

by

Genevah D. Seivertson

Based on lessons given by
Eleanore Mary Thedick
Christ Ministry Foundation

DeVorss & Company
P.O. Box 550
Marina del Rey, California 90291

Copyright © 1981
by Genevah D. Seivertson

⁷/₀₂

ISBN: 0-87516-465-X
Library of Congress Card Catalog Number:81-69023

Printed in the United States of America
by Book Graphics, Inc., California

∨

This book is lovingly dedicated
to all who minister "In His Name"

with especial appreciation
to my husband, Wayne, and
my Sacramento 'girls' who
undergirded me

The Bible quotations are from the King James Version

THE CHRIST HIGHWAY

"And a Highway shall be there and
a Way, and it shall be called the
Way of Holiness" (Isaiah: 35:8)

CONTENTS

Eleanore Mary Thedick

(1883–1973)

Eleanore Mary Thedick was a twentieth century mystic and visionary, known in the angelic world as "The Messenger." Her complete devotion to Christ Jesus as she called our Lord, kept her path true, simple and constant.

Born in England in 1883, she and her soon-widowed mother came to America shortly after the turn of the century. Even as a child she was filled with a deep curiosity about spiritual things for which no one had the answers.

While still young, visions began to develop for her. Slowly she got inner guidance as well as proper training from others for her obvious gifts.

She lived out more than fifty years of her life in modest circumstances in Oakland, California. She was always available to those who were drawn to her but never sought publicity nor grandeur.

Her teachings take the extraordinary wonder of Christianity and make it available in an acceptable, ordinary manner.

Introduction

"Many rivers run into the sea. If you see God as the sea, you will know that different religions are the rivers. All religions come to the same Godhead with different methods of getting there."
> Master Hilarian to Eleanore Mary
> Thedick in the 1930's.

The river which ran into the sea of God for Eleanore Mary Thedick was actually an upward, curving road that she named The Christ Highway. Others were drawn to travel with her through the classes she taught, the books which were written and the personal contact of prayer or counseling. Some students were with her only a time or two; others for years.

Either way, they remembered the one who was willing to help them along their special way while she continued to climb the route so clearly marked for her. That highway included almost daily communication with heavenly beings for Mrs. Thedick saw angels. She talked to them. They spoke to her. As "The Messenger," she relayed their lessons and advice.

The extra-ordinary became ordinary in the life of Eleanore Thedick for she easily balanced her relationship with angels and with people. "The advice that the angels give," she would tell her students, "is sensible and helpful. If this is so, why not listen, whether or not we can see them? When we read a book, we don't see the author, but we listen to what is said. Angels are as real as the author.

"Angels are as real as the people in another town or country whom we cannot see, but whose existence we accept. We form an opinion about them from what we hear and read. Sometimes we meet them in person. Just so with angelic forces. We find out about them through reading and listening. Sometimes we may meet them in person.

"Angels are as much as part of our Father's world as we are. We can let them assist us or not. The choice is ours."

Eleanore Thedick chose to listen and thus published four booklets. She claimed title to only one of them, an autobiography. "How can I say I'm the author of the others?" she often said. "I only wrote down what was told to me."

It could have been easy for her not to have written down the messages she heard, for Eleanore Thedick was very much a part of the human world. She raised two sons, cared for an ailing mother, tended her home. She was alert to happenings in her neighborhood and city, the nation and the world. She reacted, however, to current events as a traveler on The Christ Highway for she could not leave her path.

She said, "We live in two worlds, the seen or physical, and the unseen or spiritual. There is a door that leads into the unseen which opens occasionally as we cultivate reverence, love and service. When this door opens, we have a vision of a wonderful world beyond our five senses.

"We may call it a dream, but this is a glimpse of reality, for we are spiritual beings made in the image of our Creator. This physical world which seems so permanent passes quickly, but the spiritual remains eternally the same and eternally beautiful. It would not be good for us if this door remained open because we are here to learn lessons on the physical plane that we could not learn anywhere else.

"This door has opened just a little for me and sometimes I hear the voice of the Teacher with my inner ear or I see a beautiful vision with my inner eye. I want to share these visions and teachings with you."

She does this in *The Christ Highway*, her first basic book and the other three which followed. The disciplines used to travel the road to Christ Consciousness are given step by step.

The teachings of lessons 1 through 36 are succinct. The purpose of this enlarged text is to expand the scope of the original booklet with additional teachings and examples of practical application.

Special Prayers

Certain prayers of protection were given to Eleanore Mary Thedick. She taught that it is very necessary to clothe ourselves in these prayers as outer garments to start each day's adventures. We are vulnerable when we become still and are willing to listen to the guidance of the Holy Spirit. Disturbing thoughts can reach us at the same time when we are thus open. The powerful vibrations of these prayers asking the Christ Spirit to protect us will sift the thoughts and emotions which approach us and ward off negative thoughts and actions.

We have placed these prayers here at the beginning of the lessons so you may become familiar with them and begin to experience their benefits. Used often and frequently, they become tools of power and deliverance. Each prayer is considered in more detail in the lessons.

Prayers of Protection

The wall of flame

"In the Name, through the Power, and by the Word of the Living Christ, I build a wall of flame around myself, my loved ones, my home, my affairs and any conveyance I

1

may use. I give grateful thanks for this protection.
Amen."

This affirmation is based on the Bible verse from
Zechariah 2:5. Reading Zechariah 2:1–5 will be beneficial
for a picture of the vastness of this protection will emerge.

Cleansing of our aura

"In the Name, through the Power and by the word of
Jesus Christ, my aura is cleansed of everything but the
pure white light of the Christ. My aura is recharged with
the same white light of the Christ."

Refer to Second Corinthians 7:1 for verification of this
prayer. The emanation of life which flows from us and en-
circles us is called our aura. All of our emotions, positive
and negative, are evidenced in this unseen reflection of
ourselves. When we use this special cleansing prayer, we
wash our emotions in much the same way we cleanse our
bodies.

The armour of light

"In the Name, through the Power and by the Word of
Christ Jesus, I put on the whole Armour of Light. On my
head is the helmet of Salvation. I wear the breastplate of
Righteousness. My loins are girded with the Truth. My
feet are shod with Peace and enveloped in the flame of the
Spirit of Almighty God. In my left hand I hold the shield
of Faith. In my right hand is the sword of Spirit.

"This is the Word of God and the Word of God is unassailable. Only Good shall come to me. Thus clad, I stand
joyfully expectant, ready to do the Will of the Father.
Amen."

This is adapted from St. Paul's letter to the Ephesians
6:11–18.

The Christ prayer

"Beloved Christ, we, thy children, close the door of the outer world and contemplate Thy Holy Presence within us.

"We feel the Christ love flowing through us. All that is unlike Thee disappears. We are infilled with Thy purifying love which supplies our spiritual and our physical needs.

"We radiate this love to all the world to bless and heal Thy children everywhere." (At this point bring to mind individuals, groups or situations which need healing.)

"We give thanks that we have received. The Word has gone forth to bless and to heal in the Name of the Living Christ.   Amen."

This prayer which was given intact to Mrs. Thedick is to be used as an integral part of each day's lesson. It will be studied in detail in lessons eight and nine.

Let the work be tempered

"In the Name of the Living Christ, let all the spiritual work done for me, by me or through me be tempered for its perfect expression."

Instructions to the Seeker

Dear Seeker:

These lessons are sign posts on the highway of life. If faithfully studied and practiced, you will gain a deeper understanding of Jesus Christ. The Christ is within you as the Christ Consciousness and without you as your Lord, Saviour and beloved Teacher.

To obtain the best results, read this book slowly, taking one lesson at a time. Follow very closely the instructions which are given to you, the seeker.

If it is your nature to read all of a book from first to last, indulge yourself, but then return to the beginning and work with the contents, session by session.

Spiritual Tools

If you are holding this book in your hands, then it is written especially for you.

If you are already well along the highway with Jesus Christ, you may stretch your horizons even farther.

If you have not quite made up your mind whether the road of the King is for you, you may get your answer.

If you are investigating the Way, you may learn much.

If you have been put off by the traditional representation of Christianity, you may find your own Christian expression in these pages.

If you are weary of either doctrine or phenomena, you can find sincerity and realness in these lessons.

This book takes Christ out of the sky and into our daily way of living. Christ Jesus lived life to the fullest and calls us to do the same. (John 10:10)

He was in deep communication with intellectuals. (Nicodemus, John 3:1, and Joseph of Arimatheus, John 19:38)

He worked with the confused. ("Legion", Mark 5:1-11)

He spoke to the wise and the foolish. (Parable of the ten virgins, Matt. 25:2-13)

He commended the generous. (The widow and two coins, Mark 12:42-43)

5

Activity was rewarded and hesitation challenged. (Parable of the talents, Matt. 25:14–30)

He respected men of faith. (The centurian, Matt. 8:5–13)

And those who doubted. (Thomas, John 20:24–29)

The diseased were made well. (The leper, Matt. 8:2–3)

The dead raised. (Lazarus, John 11:41–44)

What He did for others, He will do for us. He is willing to help us and heal us. He challenges us and disciplines us, but He promises the kingdom of God is within each one of us. (Luke 17:21)

He says He came to bring joy, forgiveness, peace, love, life, light to us.

Let us, then symbolically open our hands, our minds, our hearts, to receive these gifts as we study *The Christ Highway.*

We shall study lesson one in some detail so that you may follow a similar expanded procedure through all the lessons.

We are told in the first lesson that we have an appointment with God which should be kept every day.

Think about your own special time right now.

Is it easier to rise more early in the morning for your time apart?

Would you prefer to get early morning details finished first?

Possibly the evening is best for you?

Whatever time you choose, it is best to be consistent. The discipline will enhance you and stay with you as building blocks of power long after the exercises of the book are finished.

You will be keeping an appointment with the Christ Spirit, that mightiness which is within you as the Image and Likeness of God and without you as Creative Force.

Your guardian angel will soon adapt to your special time, alertly waiting for an invitation to work with you.

Many other angels will also be willing to join you when they discover you are seriously proceeding with your own individual work.

Your consistency and willingness to become acquainted with and more deeply aware of the Christ Spirit within you, your openness to learning more of the angelic helpers, your prayers, may help you uncover your life pattern which God planted within you long ago.

All this, you question, from studying a book, praying and having a daily quiet time? Why not? This is your own book. Let it speak to you in your own way. Discover all that is for you. Use the five senses which God has given you. Read with your eyes and your mind; hear the instructions on a deep inner level; experience the benefits as food for your body; sense on your indrawn breath your closeness to your Source; reach out and touch another with the same blessing.

As you settle down to your time you have decided upon, begin with praying the prayers of protection as given in the front of the book. The value of these prayers will become more apparent to you as you continue to work with them.

Next, take time to become absorbed in The Christ Prayer. Let yourself experience the directives. Feel yourself pulling apart from the thinking, analyzing part of yourself and the world, joining forces with the listening, hearing, sensing part of yourself and the world.

Let the feeling of unity and power contained in being of a prayerful attitude permeate you.

Read the daily statement of Lesson One.

It says, "The Christ is born in me today."

Say the words aloud.

"The Christ is born in me today."

Repeat them again.

"The Christ is born in me today."

And again.

What does this mean to you? What mental pictures

come to your mind? Do you think of a great white light containing all the wonders of wisdom and love radiating all through you? Do you see the Christ as a person within your body, waiting for you to speak to? Find your own simile.

Read all of lesson one.

Compare the thinking given there with your own ideas. Do the two agree?

If you allow it, the message will speak personally to you. Do not try to analyze. Rather, let yourself hear what is for you.

Begin to consider what particular seed of the Christ you would like to evidence in your life. Become still . . . what thoughts come to you?

Are you quick tempered and need patience?

Restless, wanting peace?

Resentful, lacking love?

This is your study.

You will know.

Make a note as to the quality or qualities which present themselves. Become willing to watch for growth.

Perhaps you may be like Nicodemus about whom you read in John 3:1–21. Mentally an intellectual giant, he was yet unable to understand that Jesus' references were not to matters of the physical, but rather of the spiritual. Let the scripture speak to you as to what is right for you, rather than for it always to continue in a regimented pattern. The words of the lesson can help this process.

After you have studied the text, answer the questions as

best you can, continuing to allow answers to unfold for you.

Next, give our Lord an opportunity to speak to you in a meditational time. Become physically comfortable, preferably in a sitting position, not slouching, back fairly erect. Put your feet flat upon the floor, taking your shoes off if your prefer.

When your feet are flat upon the floor you have an opportunity for a further process of protection. To prevent any possibility of becoming dreamlike, anchor your feet to the ground as with a magnet. Let yourself draw energy from the earth itself up through your left foot. Feel it rise up as far as the lower back. This may be a tingling sensation; a sense of earth's electricity coming into you.

Send this magnetism across the lower back and let it go down the right leg and foot, returning to the earth, thus providing you with an anchor called "grounding". Listening to the Lord in such circumstances is indeed having your "feet upon the earth and your head in the stars."

As you sit quietly, almost instinctively your arms, hands, knees and ankles will uncross. Nothing will hamper the flow of Spirit throughout your whole body. Your hands will fall easily into a natural position, perhaps upon your knees with palms gently cupped upward.

Almost without realization, you will breathe deeply. Your shoulders will begin to slacken. With each successive breath there will be a downward droop of the shoulder muscles as tension is released. Your head will gently weave from side to side upon its stem, your neck.

Your breath gradually lightens as you become more deeply engrossed in the Christ Spirit. Your jaw unclamps. Your tongue loosens. Relaxation goes on down through all of your body . . . the muscles with which you swallow . . . the chest area . . . diaphragm . . . abdominal muscles.

Your sitting muscles are easy as are your knees . . . the

calves of your legs . . . your ankles. Your heels and the
arches of your feet relax. It is as though any remaining
tenseness flows on out of your body through your toes and
finger tips.

You are at peace.

In this stillness you permit yourself to become aware of
the crown of your head, often called the I AM center. At
birth this was called your "soft spot" and it was especially
guarded for it was still open to the heavenly impulses of
the world from which you had recently come. It is through
this area the pure, white light of the Christ can enter into
you and spread throughout all of you, for there is still a
connection there.

Perhaps by words you invite the Christ Consciousness
to enter and merge with the Christ heart of you. Or there
may be a spontaneous paean of praise at the realization of
your oneness. Do you feel a warm tingling, an undulating
motion as the light from without is absorbed by the light
within?

If this is a new experience to you, take time to adjust,
but permit the expression of melding to continue.
Remember, you are well grounded with your feet on the
earth and you are protected from all but the good of God.

Realize that the Spirit of the Christ is real and active and
willing to enter into you, merging with the living Christ
which is always within you.

This white light is the wisdom of God; the very love and
life of God. It comes into you as you invite it. You can absorb the intuition of God this way; the peace of God; the
joy of God, always in perfect proportion.

As you ask for this light in your own way, be sure you
do not get too much nor too little by praying, "let the light
be tempered to my needs." Then rest easy, for God hears
our prayers and it is His desire always that you be filled
with the Spirit of the Christ, no matter how you ask.

There are other ways to become attuned with the Christ light than by invitation or praising God. Is it your way to implore? To plead? It may be natural for you to say, "Please God, if it be Your will, will you send the Christ light into and through me, tempered to what is right for me?" If so, rest easy, knowing you will receive, for it is God's desire always that you be filled with the Spirit of the Christ.

Do you speak easily from an attitude of thanksgiving? Perhaps you would say, "Thank you, God, for filling me with the pure white light of the Christ, tempered to what is right for me. I feel it pouring through me now. I thank you for using it in and through me." And it will be so.

Do you operate from a sense of doubt? Would your prayer be, "God, I'm not at all sure you can come into me from outside or even that you are inside of me. There must be a certain amount of willingness in me, though, or I wouldn't be trying this. I give you that willingness to work with. Be sure to temper whatever you send me for I don't want to be burned out by anything. Either give me the faith to believe without sensation, or let me know that you are real in some way. I think I need you, God." Honesty is a wonderful attribute and you will be respected and rewarded.

Because this is your highway, realize that wherever you are in your thinking, your own experiences will come to you. If you allow them, they will be good.

After finding yourself in the maze of possibilities, what is your reaction? Is there a feeling of warmth or tingling? A solid sense of knowing . . . of accepting . . . without any particular emotion? An acceptance through a statement of faith such as "I trust you, God"? Some way achieve a realization that the Light of the Christ enters into you through the crown of your head and will go all through you.

Creative Force from which you were formed will begin

to permeate you, touching all of the areas which you have relaxed. There is a gentle radiance in all of you. Every atom, cell, pore, sinew, muscle, every organ of you is being blessed with the healing, relaxing, learning Spirit of the Christ.

All strain and worry are gone from you. You are immersed in a cleansing rinse of Light. All that is unlike your true nature . . . the nature of God within you . . . leaves you.

These words burn themselves into your heart and mind: "Angel of Protection, I invite you in to place yourself at the door of my consciousness as I seek the path to power within myself, that I may safely travel it and wisely use it. I ask you to guard every avenue of approach to my body, mind and soul, that I alone may enter the Silence and claim my birthright of divine knowledge through the spiritual gifts which are the links between my outer and my inner levels of consciousness.

"No thought force, no outer force of any description shall enter my aura without my consent. I am filled with the Light of Christ. I am indwelled by the knowledge of what I am to learn. I am alone in the Christ Consciousness. I rest."

And you do this.

Five minutes.

Ten.

Perhaps one.

Time has no place with you.
You will know when you are ready for further learning.
You are keeping your appointment with Christ Jesus. You are aware that this is a divine appointment.

It becomes easy for you to realize that you are called to experience this book rather than read it.

There is a realization that you are imbued with The Christ Prayer with which you began this session for you have truly closed the door of the outer world.

You are contemplating the Holy presence of the Christ within you.

You are filled with love so deeply that you feel you must share.

Names of those in need come to your mind and the love of God flows out from you to them.

And you are glad.

You are thankful and you say so in your own words.

You are still.

The daily statement comes to your mind. "The Christ is born in me today." You say it aloud. Once. Again.

Is it more real to you now? Is there a new stirring? a greater vibrancy? more expectation? Do you know more surely what quality you will begin to evidence? Is there a contentment that this has been a successful time apart in which you have allowed the Christ Consiousness to indwell you?

Your own answers will come to you.

As they do and you feel you have grown as much as you want for this day, you will become more aware of your breathing and the familiar objects around you. Your time of communion with your Creator will be finished for now. Perhaps you will feel like stretching your arms or yawning. You are refreshed.

You may be led to re-read Lesson One and it will have new meaning to you. The questions at the end of the lesson will keep you challenged until you feel you are ready for Lesson Two.

This has taken you through Lesson One but it is also a guide to the rest of the book. Permit each section to speak to you in its own way for it is written with you in mind. Take as much time with each section as is right for you.

Challenge yourself to continue the growth of your own Christ seed within you, learning something new each time you study.

Remember, this book is to be experienced, not merely read. The Christ Highway is a road for travelers who move along the way.

When you are ready to leave this experience, ask that your protection be renewed with the white light of the Christ surrounding you and your feet firmly grounded.

Repeat the Lord's Prayer and carry your learnings into the day's adventure.

The Birth of the Christ

Beloved, today you have an appointment with Christ Jesus, your teacher and friend. Keep this appointment daily at the same hour, if possible. Begin your devotions by putting on the armour of Light. Commit the daily statement to memory; look up the Bible reference and read your lesson slowly. Study its meaning since it applies to your life and its problems. Ask your Lord to help you find the spirit behind the written words and then close your devotional period with a prayer for others. End with the Lord's Prayer.

THE STATEMENT

The Christ is born in me today.

John 3:2-21

Once a year the Christian world celebrates the birth of Christ Jesus, but in the individual, the birth of Christ is a mystical process and may take place at any time. In our Bible reference, you will notice that Christ Jesus used the same method that all advanced teachers of mystical truths use, symbology, which is the language of the higher planes. The Master recognized Nicodemus as an advanced spiritual teacher and addressed him in the language of symbols, but Nicodemus failed to understand Him.

Our Lord tells us very plainly that God is our Father and that this Father dwells within each human being in a mental state called "The Kingdom of Heaven." As St. Paul reminds us in 2nd Corinthians 6:16, "God has said of you, 'I will live in them and walk among them.'"

Like the human child we inherit His attributes from our Father, but they are in embryo or seed form. They require a birth, or a coming forth, before they can be expressed in this outer consciousness or material existence. The focusing of the Christ-power of Divine Love in the life of the individual has the same growing effect as the rays of the sun in the physical world. This Divine Love has the power to bring forth these seeds we call peace, health, joy, love and all that we name God or good into expression in our lives.

Name your Christ that is born in you today as Christ-life, Christ-peace, Christ-love, Christ-health or whatever you desire to be born or brought forth in you. It is easier for the one who is seeking spiritual unfoldment to understand and follow the law of nature which is seed, growth, flower and harvest. All of these seeds, these attributes of God lie within your heart, but you must be willing to unfold these spiritual blossoms slowly.

The most wonderful things in life are not quickly or easily won. Soul blossoms seem slow in their unfolding to our finite way of thinking because of their very nature. All seed is alive and according to the law of life, must come forth some time or other.

There are two ways in which the seed comes forth or is born. One is the slow and difficult way of experience, which is sowing, reaping or cause and effect. The other way is easier for it is the Christ Way . . . the Way of Grace. It is recognizing this indwelling power and working consciously with it.

Beloved, is it health, peace, joy or abundance that you are seeking to bring forth? Name your seed today, for your words are Spirit and they shall not return to you void. Never mind appearances. Speak your word in confidence and with faith and leave the rest to your Lord, Christ Jesus. Go even further back to the Prophet Isaiah who tells us the Father says, "I am the Lord, thy God, that teacheth thee to profit; which leadeth thee in the way thou shouldest go." (Isa. 48:17)

QUESTIONS ON DAILY LESSON ONE

1. *Why is it necessary to study your lesson at the same time daily?*
2. *What brings the God-attributes forth in the individual?*
3. *Why should you name your Christ seed?*
4. *In spiritual unfoldment, what is the law to follow?*
5. *Why should spiritual blossoms unfold slowly?*
6. *Explain how the seed of God-life comes forth.*
7. *What is appearance?*

The Faith of the Christ

Beloved, keep your appointment faithfully day by day with Jesus Christ, your teacher and friend. Take these seven steps daily.

(1) First, protect yourself by putting on the "Armour of Light" and then begin your communion with your Lord by using the Christ Prayer.
(2) Memorize your Daily Statement.
(3) Read the Bible reference carefully and study it.
(4) Ask for light from the Giver of Light, your own indwelling Christ.
(5) Read your lesson slowly. Study it well for it is a personal message from Jesus Christ to you.
(6) Take half an hour daily, no longer, for meditation.
(7) Always close your devotions with the Lord's Prayer.

THE STATEMENT

I have faith in the Living Christ

Luke 12:22–32

One of the foundation stones in the teachings of Jesus Christ is faith or belief. The definition of belief is to hope with confidence or to trust in another. We place our faith in the material side of life and then wonder why we fail to get results. We ask for things instead of cultivating the faith that brings the things into manifestation.

By what method did Jesus always get results? How did He do it? Read John 6:1-13. When Jesus fed the five thousand, His disciples told Him there was a lack and suggested several methods to overcome it, but Jesus issued a definite command. He said, "Tell them to sit down." This is the *first step* in bringing forth your desired good. Stop running around and looking to the outer world for help.

Notice carefully the *second step*. He took the small quantity He had and gave thanks. For what? The little He had? No, beloved, for the realization of abundant supply to feed all those gathered there.

The *third step* is the acting out of your inward faith or belief. He gave of the bread and fish to the waiting people and they were so abundantly supplied with food that there was a lot left over.

In John 11:1-46, we see the same three steps taken by Jesus to bring Lazarus to life. First . . . command . . . "Take ye away the stone." Take away those hard, stony states of consciousness that prevent the seed from coming forth. Second . . . the prayer of thanksgiving . . . "Father, I thank Thee that Thou has heard me". This is gratitude and recognition of the divine relationship. Third . . . acting upon the assurance that He has received His answer . . . "Lazarus, come forth" which is a positive, definite word.

We are His beloved and we must follow in His steps when we want to bring forth the Christ seed, whether it is health, joy or supply. Remember the three steps necessary to bring forth that seed. *First* . . . cease outer efforts like running around and looking to people and things for help. *Second* . . . always remember to pray the prayer of rejoicing that you *now* have, not will have, your desire.

Third . . . have faith to act as if it were true, and that your desire has already come forth in this physical world.

Thanksgiving and rejoicing is the law or avenue by which your good is brought forth into manifestation. All of God's good for you is already in the inner waiting for the call of faith or belief to bring it into expression.

"Ye believe in God, believe also in me." (John 14:1)

Peace be with you.

QUESTIONS ON DAILY LESSON TWO

1. *Name one foundation stone in the teachings of Jesus Christ.*
2. *Why do we fail to get our desires?*
3. *What three steps did Jesus take to demonstrate?*
4. *What state of consciousness is necessary to bring forth your good?*
5. *What effect has gratitude and thanksgiving on your demonstration?*
6. *Why should we enjoy our good mentally before we receive it?*
7. *What message does Jesus Christ leave with us in this lesson?*

The Growth of the Christ

Beloved, be faithful in keeping your daily appointment with your Lord Jesus Christ. The repeating of the Christ Prayer and the reading of the Bible reference help you build a beautiful temple of spiritual power. This is a place of meeting between you and your Lord, the secret place of the most high.

THE STATEMENT

I am growing more Christlike daily.

Matt. 13:23

Let us go into the garden of our hearts with the divine gardener this morning. Winter is still holding sway there and everything seems dead and desolate. This is only an appearance, however, for underneath this so-called death is life awaiting the call to come forth and express.

See how the divine gardener cuts away the rank growth so withered and dry, those outgrown, discarded ideas, thoughts and deeds of yesterday. This pruning always takes place in your life and mine, beloved, and it would be less painful if we were more nonresistant. We must be more willing to let go and let God work in and through us.

We close our hands tightly around our loved ones and our affairs instead of placing them in the hands of the loving Christ. And the little seed that we planted in the garden of our hearts, where is it? Will it ever show above the ground of material conditions? Yes, there is a tiny plant showing in the garden, but something is wrong for we can hardly find it.

Surrounding the little plant, shadowing it from the sun, crowding it out of its rightful place is the husky little weed called "fear." With fear and doubt in our minds, we begin to say, "I don't feel much better." "I wonder if I am doing right." or "I'll never get it done."

These lusty weeds have many names but they all spring from the same root . . . ignorance. We know them only too well as fear, envy, worry, selfishness and their vast family. They spring up in every heart's garden, crowding out the flowers.

What must we do with them? Why, pull them up, root and branch, and plant the opposite. Substitute faith for fear, peace for worry, love for envy and service for selfishness. Repeat over and over again, "I have faith in Christ. My faith is strong," until the Angel of Faith, hearing his name called so often, comes to your heart to stay.

Our work is to remove the weeds and plant flowers in our heart's garden. We must surround the little seed with hope and expectation as in the statement from Psalms 62:5, "My soul, wait thou only upon God for my expectation is from Him."

Sometimes the ground is stony (hard states of consciousness) and then we have harrowing experiences that dig deep into our hearts. Let us rejoice when we meet these hard experiences and know that in this way the ground is being prepared for the tiny plant. As it grows, it becomes a thing of beauty and brings forth the fruits of peace, love, joy, health and abundant supply. Truly, "the desert shall rejoice and blossom as a rose." (Isa. 35:1)

Peace be with you.

Questions on Daily Lesson Three

1. *As we study and meditate, what are we gradually building?*
2. *What rank growth must first be cut away?*
3. *How can we help in getting rid of this growth?*
4. *What is the root of all weeds?*
5. *Name some flowers used to substitute for the weeds.*
6. *How can we promote the growth of our seeds?*
7. *Tests will come as we plant our seeds. How shall we meet them?*

Meeting Your Personal Christ

Are you surprised that your prayers of protection, your exercise of grounding yourself and asking that the work of power be tempered, as well as the Christ Prayer have not prevented the emotional weeds of anger, discontent and pride from being cultivated in your garden of life? Ah, but these characteristics were there long before you started the prayers! The prayers have probably brought the frustrations and worries to mind. It's easy, then, to recognize them as weeds to be dealt with.

As you know your needs, getting rid of them is as near as allowing the Christ Spirit within you to be enhanced by the great Christ Force of the universe. This power exists now, always has existed and always will. It is eternal . . . everlasting. Because of this, there is no part of us, old or young, big or small which cannot be touched and healed.

When we work in a tangible garden of flowers, we often get thorns in our hands which hurt and fester if not removed. Worry, envy, fear, hatred and resentment are some of the thorns in our garden of life. They also hurt and fester if not removed. Sometimes we can remove the thorns from our fingers or hands by ourselves and that is good. Sometimes we have to go to a physician and that, too, is good.

Sometimes we can remove the negative feelings from

our body and soul by ourselves and that is good. Sometimes we have to go to the Great Physician . . . God . . . through the Christ Spirit . . . and that also is good.

Are you willing to let the Christ Spirit remove your thorns? Take time to muse a bit about your willingness. Think also how Jesus Christ becomes real to *you* for this is an individual experience.

Do you communicate with Jesus Christ as a being who has personality; that is actually a person with whom you can speak?

Or is the Christ a part of the Godhead which mediates for the human race?

Perhaps the Christ Spirit is an all-enveloping, overwhelming, yet still available outpouring of All-Good.

Whatever your conviction is in regard to the Christ Spirit, that is the power which is available to you.

The Bible tells us that Jesus Christ appeared in different ways to different people after His resurrection. Mary Magdalene thought He was a gardener for a while (John 20:15). The two men on the road to Emmaus felt He was a fellow traveler till He broke bread with them (Luke 24:16). In like manner, He will walk with you and work with you in the way which is acceptable to you.

As you have become willing, you will know your own version of this Son of God who has returned to the Godhead and you realize that He is your own Lord who is willing to work for and with you.

It is time, then, to give the Christ the opportunity to help you with those thorns in your garden of life which have been too much for you to deal with.

You learned a way to become still and meditate in the section called "Spiritual Tools" (page 5). Prepare to do this now, by using the prayers of protection and the Christ Prayer and asking that the work you are doing shall be tempered for you. Let yourself relax until you feel no outside influence. You are at one with your Creative Force.

Speak now to your Christ as you know Him. Invite Him to come within you as helper, healer, friend. Explain where you are in your own feelings. Speak words aloud, for there is power in the spoken word which is not there as much in silent thought. The spoken word goes out into space, into the part of God which surrounds us as air and vibrates with power. Mention the thorns of which you have become aware that keep you from expressing your highest good.

If there are persons against whom you hold a grudge, tell the Christ about this. Have you been injured physically, spiritually or in your feelings and haven't been able to forgive? Mention these things. Let everything which comes easily to your mind be brought out.

You may then think of incidents from the past. Pour out your feelings about them, confident that our Lord will accept what you are saying in love. He already knows, for nothing is hidden from Him, and He is pleased to have you become aware.

When the first rush of feeling is past and you think you are done with your sharing, tell our Lord these things:

1. You haven't been able to deal with things you have told Him about or you would have done so.

2. There may be other memories hidden in your subconscious mind that you can't or won't remember which also need healing.

3. You recognize that the Christ Spirit which is always alight in you is forged with the Christ Spirit from without which has poured into you when you invited it.

4. You know that eternal Christ Spirit can cleanse and heal as it is allowed.

5. You are able . . . right at this moment . . . to grant permission for this cleansing, forgiving, healing experience to take place within you.

And it is so.

Your confidence in Jesus Christ as you know Him allows you to open yourself more widely than ever before for cleansing and forgiving and healing. Where are you in life at this moment?

Retired?

At the peak of your working years?

A homemaker?

Are you middle-aged?

A parent or grandparent?

A son or daughter?

Are you a young adult?

In college?

A teenager?

Start wherever you are, dividing your life into sections of time according to the groups above, but leading on back into your childhood and even to your time of conception. Allow yourself time in each area, letting each era bring its own memories. You are safe because you have asked that the work be tempered and no emotion will be more than you can bear, though you may be moved to tears.

Are you troubled in your retirement? Do you feel neglected by your family; unappreciated by your mate; financially insecure? Have you become irritable? Have you hurt the feelings of your family and friends?

In this place of life or any other that you are, the healing begins as you let the power of the Christ act. Scenes you have not thought about for years play themselves out before your eyes. You are aware that your feelings were badly hurt; that you have not been able to forgive those who injured you. It is too big for you! The results are too shocking!

You cannot forgive, but the Christ can. He can overwhelm you with the knowledge that your buried resentment eats at you, not the other person, and you suddenly know the price of resentment, or jealousy, or hatred is too great to pay. You become willing to let the Christ wash your memory clean. And you rest.

This goes over and over, through all of your life, starting where you are now, working backward through all of your years. Each era of your life is washed clean. It is good.

You become aware, also, that there are places where you have done wrong and that you have not asked for forgiveness, nor even been sorry. Many of the people are no longer where you could contact them. Many would not appreciate your stirring the mud of the past. But your heart is heavy.

Let it lighten! Let the Christ walk through all of your life, lifting the load of guilt from you. His burden is so easy that you hand everything to Him and you forgive yourself. Say aloud, "With the help of my own Christ, I forgive myself! He forgives me and I forgive me!"

Let joy and peace and wholeness fill all of you. Take time to revel in the grace of accepting right answers . . . receive . . . believe . . . relax . . . enjoy freedom . . . rejoice . . . give thanks!

Your heart swells in appreciation. You recognize that all of God is within you. You are made in His Image and Likeness. You are grateful that you are willing for the best of you to shine forth.

Become ready, now, to participate once more in life by renewing your protection, by asking that the pure white light of the Christ surround you. Make sure your feet are firmly on the ground.

Pray the Lord's Prayer.

You may need to rest a bit for much has been done in your life. You need time to assimilate.

You are all new!

The Christ Love (I)

Beloved, if you look forward with joy to this daily communion with Jesus Christ, then His joy will fill your heart. When you repeat the Christ Prayer which is part of each day's pattern, you are linking up with the Hosts of Heaven. You are adding your light to the radiance of the Christ light and you are bringing brightness into your life and the lives of those around you. The Master says to you today, "Let *your* light so shine." (Matt. 5:16)

THE STATEMENT

I love everybody with the Love of Christ.

John 17:1–26

The most beautiful flower in the garden of our hearts is the rose of divine love. The bringing forth of this Christ blossom of love is the crowning achievement in the human life. Jesus Christ was often called the "Master of Love," because He was love embodied. He brought the gift of divine love to this world and His entire ministry was a service of love.

In our Bible reading today is the beautiful prayer that

Christ prayed for us all. You and I are especially mentioned in verse 20. Read this verse carefully. As we realize dimly how much He loves us, we want to express more love for Him. How can we do this? The Christ gives and we receive, so to have more love, we must give more love.

The first step in the unfolding of the rose of divine love is to correct our thoughts and think more lovingly toward all. This is like broadcasting over a spiritual radio for our thoughts go out to another just like radio waves go out through space.

We are becoming more and more aware that every thought we think reaches the person or thing we have in mind so we will benefit if, like Jesus Christ, we include "all" in our loving thoughts and prayers.

Broadcast thoughts of love over the spiritual radio, especially to those who have treated you unkindly, for unkind thoughts will antagonize them. Say silently to them, "I love you with the love of Jesus Christ." Do not forget your lesser brothers of the natural world, the animals and the birds. Take time to send out love thoughts to the natural kingdom and all its inhabitants. It is unthinkable to us that the great Master of love would not express His healing love to the lesser forms of life as well as the greater.

We who follow in His steps must always remember to send out the Christ love to the lesser creations over whom we have been given dominion. "Thou madest him to have dominion over the works of Thy hands." (Ps. 8:6) Our loving thoughts sent out into space, when linked to the One Name, have a power we little dream of. Our part is not to weigh, measure or discuss the power. We must link up with it by the use of the One Name, and leave the rest in higher hands than ours. "For there is none other name under heaven given among men, whereby we must be saved." (Acts 4:12)

A great teacher of spiritual laws told his students that

one loving thought sent to a single butterfly was felt by each one of them. Our lesser brothers are very sensitive to love vibrations. We help ourselves as well as others by just thinking loving thoughts in the Name of Jesus Christ to all creation.

"Beloved, if God so loved us, we ought also to love one another." (I John 4:11)

Peace be with you.

QUESTIONS ON DAILY LESSON FOUR

1. *What is the most beautiful flower in the garden of our hearts?*
2. *How can we express more love for Christ?*
3. *Why should we send loving thoughts to the other creations?*
4. *Who was called the "Master of love?"*
5. *What Name must we link up with?*
6. *To get results must we analyze the power of that Name?*
7. *How do we help ourselves and others?*

The Christ Love (II)

Beloved, during the study of these lessons on the Christ love which is the heart of these teachings, try to realize that the great Master of love is your constant companion. At any time you may make connection or tune in to His consciousness and actually feel waves of golden light flooding your entire being. These waves indicate His presence.

THE STATEMENT

The Christ love is now active in me.

John 15:9–27

Let us pick up the threads from our last lesson on how to bring forth the rose of divine love in our heart's garden. A great psychologist has said, "Under all circumstances, keep an even mind." The Christ says to you, that you should be loving under all circumstances. (Read Matthew, chapters 5 and 6.) We will never realize the healing power of divine love until we learn to use it to adjust and harmonize the tangled threads of our own lives.

Take your little seed of health, for instance. To bring it
forth, you must bless and love every organ in your
wonderful body. Love releases the inner healing power
and allows it to flow unobstructed through the body. Hate
or fear, the opposite or negative vibration, tightens and
tenses the whole physical organism and obstructs the healing flow. Pour the 'oil of love', divine love, on any
adverse condition and you will overcome it. If you find
yourself dreading to meet a certain person or condition,
pave the way for an harmonious meeting by sending
thoughts of love ahead of you.

Never make the statement, "I hate to do this," for
words are living things which return to the creator to be
redeemed. Matthew 12:36 says it this way, "Every idle
word that men shall speak, they shall give account
thereof." You will fasten a condition to you with steel-like
bands if you hate it. Always use love to heal inharmony.
Be non-resistant to so-called evil. Close your eyes to the
appearance of evil in the lives of others. Magnify the good
and see the Christ coming forth in them. Make it a habit to
think lovingly toward life.

At first you will have to watch yourself very closely.
Unloving thoughts and words will try to come forth, but
you must heal them with love. This is not easy, beloved,
but the easy thing has no real value. If you will meditate
upon the love of Christ every day you will find a new,
kind, tolerant and forgiving spirit coming forth in you.
People and circumstances that seemed rasping will have
lost their power to annoy. This is the great remedy. Try it.

For example, take any adverse condition in your own
personal life and think and act lovingly toward it for the
next thirty days. The results will surprise you. Do not
think hate or fear thoughts one minute and love thoughts
the next, for such thoughts bring partial success and partial failure. "For as he thinketh in his heart, so is he."
(Prov. 23:7)

To strengthen the thought of love, write the words of the daily statement many times and read the greatest treatise on love ever written. This is found in First Corinthians, chapter 13. "There is no fear in love but perfect love casteth out fear." (I John 4:18)

Peace be with you.

Questions on Daily Lesson Five

1. *Is there any special time when one can "tune in" to the Christ Consciousness?*
2. *What indicates the presence of Christ?*
3. *What must we do to realize the healing power of divine love?*
4. *What fastens conditions to you?*
5. *What habit must you form?*
6. *How can one get rid of adverse conditions?*
7. *What is the result of mixing constructive and destructive thoughts?*

The Christ Forgiveness

Beloved, the words you read are only the avenue that Christ Jesus is using to bring you closer to Him. He desires to help, comfort and teach you. According to your faith will be the results.

Take a few minutes after you repeat the Christ Prayer to send the forgiving thought to everyone who has tried in any way to hurt you. Bless each one of them in the Name of Jesus Christ.

THE STATEMENT

I forgive others as freely as Jesus Christ forgives me.
Matt. 18:21-35

Forgiveness plays a large part in the teachings of Jesus. He places no limit on the number of times we must forgive others. In reading Matt. 5:23-24, we see that before we can expect to receive from our heavenly Father, we must be at peace with our human brother. We must forgive him for what he has done to us. It does not matter to the loving Christ how many times we have denied Him and turned to follow our own willful way. He forgives us freely and fully in the moment we turn to Him, and even before that. "Before they call I will answer." (Isa. 65:24)

To grow in the consciousness of the indwelling Christ, we must forgive others. It is also necessary that we forgive ourselves just as freely. Negative attitudes of blame, condemnation and self-depreciation result in what psychologists call complexes.

We all know that these complexes finally work out into negative conditions in our bodies. Self-pity and self-depreciation are only modern names for the same old weeds that we are trying to uproot in the garden of our hearts. We worked with uprooting these in daily lesson three and in the section called "Meeting your Personal Christ." Therefore, the next time you start condemning or blaming yourself, stop and ask this question: "Who am I blaming?"

Jesus said, "Be ye therefore perfect, even as your Father which is in heaven is perfect." (Matt. 5:48) This Father in heaven is our indwelling consciousness of divinity. Jesus also said, "Judge not that ye be not judged." (Matt. 7:1) Beloved, before you sleep tonight think of those who have hurt you or been unkind in any way. Tell them mentally that you forgive them and then bless them with the love of Jesus Christ.

Be sure and do the same for yourself. Forgive your own mistakes of the past in the Name of Christ. Think how much He forgave. As you fall asleep, let the words of the daily statement ring in your ears. "I forgive everyone as freely as Jesus Christ forgives me." You will awaken refreshed, happier and with more peace in your heart than you have felt for a long time. A load will be lifted and you will have taken a step forward.

"Be ye kind one to another, tender-hearted, forgiving one another, even as God, for Christ's sake, hath forgiven you." (Eph. 4:32)

Peace be with you.

QUESTIONS ON DAILY LESSON SIX

1. *What must we do before we can expect to receive from God?*
2. *Why must we forgive ourselves as well as others?*
3. *Give the modern names for weeds in our heart's garden.*
4. *Explain the method found in Daily Lesson Three.*
5. *Where is our Father in heaven?*
6. *What should you do before you fall asleep at night?*
7. *How do you forgive your own mistakes?*

The Peace of the Christ

INSTRUCTION TO THE SEEKER: DAILY LESSON SEVEN

Beloved, seven is a holy, peaceful number meaning spiritual instruction. It is also the Sabbath Day of rest and peace, so it is fitting that the seventh lesson should be on peace. Try to be at peace within and without today. Remain out of doors if possible and listen to the heartbeat of nature. It is found in the song of the birds, the wind in the trees and the beat of the waves on the beach.

THE STATEMENT

I rest in the peace of Christ

John 14:15–31

In the Old Testament, the number seven is mentioned a great deal. Those were the days of spiritual instructions, lessons and tests. They paved the way for the Lord Christ, the Prince of Peace, who brought the gift of peace to a troubled world. Today we find the same thing taking place in our hearts. As we forgive, a wave of peace seems to flood our entire being. The words of the Christ become personal to us. "My peace I give unto you." (John 14:27)

Peace is another name for stillness. We must get very still mentally; cease our clamor and wait upon the Lord with joy and expectation. Often it is necessary to speak to our troublesome thoughts that rush to and fro. The Master spoke to the angry waves, "Peace be still." (Mark 4:39) Very often we put too much personal force out in trying to bring forth the little seeds of our desires. "Delight thyself also in the Lord and He shall give thee the desires of thine heart." (Ps. 37:4)

Beloved, to grow and unfold spiritually, it is necessary that we have a quiet time daily with the Lord. We must practice His presence just as faithfully as we would practice singing if we desired to become a singer. This practice should not be a hardship nor should it be overdone. Let us learn to use reason and judgment in our spiritual studies as we do in our everyday life.

What did Jesus do? He had periods of prayer and then He went out and did His great works . . . infilling and outflowing. Beloved, don't you see that it is the rhythm of the universe, receiving and giving out, ebb and flow? A daily meditation and communion with your beloved Lord Jesus Christ, lasting not more than half an hour is absolutely essential for soul growth.

This half hour should be divided into part prayer and part study. Our lesson on prayer will go more fully into this. We are like harps; too much sitting in the Silence tends to loosen the strings and we become negative. Too much activity in the outer, neglecting the quiet periods and we become too tense. All health whether of body, mind or affairs is the result of harmonious adjustment.

"Acquaint now thyself with Him and be at peace: thereby good shall come unto thee." (Job 22:21)

Peace be with you.

Questions on Daily Lesson Seven

1. *What is the spiritual meaning of the number seven?*
2. *Give another name for peace.*
3. *Can we use too much personal force?*
4. *What will a "quiet time" bring forth?*
5. *How did Jesus keep in tune with the Infinite?*
6. *What is the result of too much meditation?*
7. *What is another name for health?*

Meeting the Angels

How do you respond to the suggestion that your quiet time with our beloved Lord be about thirty minutes? Do you ask, "How can I ever stay still for that long?" Or, "Where will I find the time?" Perhaps you think, "I don't want to limit myself to so little time!" Possibly thirty minutes seems just right?

It is not the ticking of the clock which is important, but rather the sense of moderation instead of extremity; of balance between time spent in meditation and living in the daily world.

Once more, take time to remember that this experience is yours alone. Perhaps you need a little more time than thirty minutes; perhaps a little less, but it is wise to find the balance between too much and too little time in the Silence. Too much time and you become involved in the phenomena of the experience and do not live out your life in the world of today. Too little time and you do not benefit from the guidance that can come.

There is a harmony in all of life. To keep our body at its peak capacity, we tense our muscles and then relax them. We breathe in; we breathe out. We listen for a while and then in turn, we speak. We work and we rest. We express beauty and balance in this way. The quiet of meditation and the activity of expression are a part of that same beauty and balance. This is true in the physical world and the spiritual world.

We have mentioned two groups of angels to you: the Angels of Protection whom we call upon every day to keep harm away from us and our Guardian Angel who is ready and waiting to help, when invited to do so. Have you become familiar with any of these angels? Had a sense of their presence? Have you invited them to help you, or spoken to them?

We are seeking beauty and balance in our expression at this time and there is a group of angels who devote their time to this work. They are called simply, the Angels of Beauty and Balance. If you ask them, they will share your devotional time and help you know when enough time is enough.

Angels are mentioned in the Bible from beginning to end; from Genesis 3:24 to Revelation 22:16. There is no actual mention of the Angels of Beauty and Balance, but if you look ahead to Daily Lesson Thirty, you will find that Angel Musicians, Angel Singers, Children's Angels and Protecting Angels, among others, are mentioned. It seems logical to believe, then, that angels are looking out for every area of our lives, especially when many groups make themselves known to us.

Psalm 91:11 tells us, "for He shall give His angels charge over thee to keep thee in all thy ways." Surely we need guidance in the area of beauty and balance. Shall we permit His angels of this area, then, to keep us on our way as we meditate today and every day?

We should concur with John Calvin who says, "Angels are the dispensers and administrators of the divine beneficence toward us. They regard our safety, undertake our defence, direct our ways, and exercise a constant solicitude that no evil befall us." (Volume I, Institutes of the Christian Religion) To do so would give us assistance in establishing the exact right amount of time for us to be in meditation and help us get every thing out of that communion that is possible.

If you would like to give angels credence in your life, you might talk to them in this manner: "Angels of Beauty and Balance, I haven't been able to see you but I am beginning to feel that angels really do exist.

"I've been told that you can give me a better balance in my approach to life. I'm not sure I thought there was anything wrong with my approach, but I'm sure you can improve it. Am I too conservative as you see me? Too liberal? Too middle-of-the-road? I've been content where I am, but I'm willing to improve.

"How shall I regard you? I'm asking you for help and I do that sometimes with my family and friends. Can we have a relationship like family or friends? How can you really help me? Will I hear a voice? See you? Will my thoughts be changed without my realization?

"I am told that you should be invited to work with and for me. I always thought you would just take care of me automatically, but when I think about it, I know I really wouldn't like you to take over my life without my permission, so I am grateful that you wait to be asked.

"As I speak, you do seem to become more real to me and I am glad. Somehow, you *do* make me feel like you are here and willing and anxious to help me. I'll be quiet now and let you work with and through me."

As you have been able to follow through on this experience, there is an awareness as you claim it. Be still now and spend some time in appreciation of your new experience for it is new, whether or not you have spoken to angels before. You are a new person from all of your learnings and every day is a new day, each experience a new one, just as we will let it be.

The Christ Prayer (I)

"Lord, teach us to pray," the disciples said to Jesus (Luke 11:1) and the same cry goes out today. In this lesson, the Lord Jesus Christ teaches you how to pray. Beloved, open your heart, sit at His feet and learn how to pray.

THE STATEMENT

Thy will is done in me today.   *Matt. 6:5-13*

Let us review the Master's words on prayer. He said, "When thou prayest, enter into thy closet, and when thou hast shut thy door, pray to thy Father which is in secret, and thy Father which seeth in secret shall reward thee openly." (Matt. 6:6) Jesus Christ could not have meant a literal room, a closet or any special place, but an area apart. He prayed under the stars; out in the open. Listen to His words, "The hour cometh and now is, when the true worshippers shall worship the Father in spirit and in truth." (John 4:23)

To "enter the closet" means to retire mentally from the outer things by closing them out of your life temporarily. Many people find the shutting of the door of thought very difficult. Trivial and wayward ideas come rushing in the

45

very moment they try to get quiet. This disturbs their
peace and they fail to contact thy Holy presence. Many
students miss the third part of the instruction on prayer
for Jesus gives three definite steps.

First step: "Enter thy closet." Retire from all outer activity. Sit or lie down, rest or be still.

Second step: "And when thou hast shut thy door." Put
out of your mind all material thoughts. Sometimes the
repeating of one of the old gospel hymns will be sufficient
to turn the current of your thoughts to spiritual things.

Third step: "Pray to your Father in secret." What does
prayer mean? It is communion, a fellowship or union
with God. Talking face to face with God . . . your God.
"With thanksgiving, let your requests be known unto
God." (Phil. 4:6)

It is a well known fact that you can keep your mind
from wandering if you will talk to your God in a soft, low
undertone. Speak the words aloud, even if you must
whisper them. The speaking of the words aloud will keep
your mind centered upon what you are doing. The Christ
Prayer has been given for our daily use. It is an example of
a perfect prayer. We know better than to plead or beseech
God, for true prayer consists of soul communion with our
Father in heaven. Before we even call, He has heard and
answered.

We have confidence and assurance that His will which is
good will, is now being done in our lives. Never forget to
praise and thank the loving God that He has heard you.
Praise and thanksgiving is the avenue over which your
good comes to you.

Should we ask for special things? Beloved, ask and rejoice that the Christ in you is now coming forth in all His
glory. "Seek ye first the kingdom of God (a consciousness
of union with your Lord) and all these things will be added
unto you." (Matt. 6:33)

Peace be with you.

QUESTIONS ON DAILY LESSON EIGHT

1. *Explain the meaning of "enter thy closet."*
2. *What is the first step in learning to pray?*
3. *What is the second step?*
4. *What is the third step?*
5. *How can we keep our mind from wandering?*
6. *What power has praise and thanksgiving?*
7. *Should we ask for special things?*

The Christ Prayer (II)

Beloved, this Christ Prayer was given direct from the high planes of consciousness. Each sentence has its own special meaning which is explained in this lesson. Meditate upon each one of them. Ask the loving Lord to reveal the inner meaning of the words to you. Divine revelation is not the property of any one person. The Christ lives within you as your divine wisdom. He is ready and waiting the call of your recognition to come forth and reveal all things to you.

THE STATEMENT

I bless all the world in the Name of Jesus Christ.
                                        Matt. 5:1–19

In our last lesson we studied prayer and its relation to us. The Christ Prayer has been given to us for our special use so let us study it. This prayer is divided into four parts. Number four means a foundation. Whenever you find this number in the Bible, it means that a foundation of some kind is being built.

48

The Christ Prayer

"Beloved Christ:

We, Thy children, close the door of the outer world and contemplate Thy holy presence within us.

We feel the Christ love flowing through us. All that is unlike Thee disappears. We are filled with Thy purifying love which supplies our spiritual and physical needs.

We radiate this love to all the world to bless Thy children everywhere. (Here think of those for whom you would like to pray; those in need or situations that need clearing up.)

We give thanks that we have received. The word has gone forth to bless and to heal in the Name of the living Christ.   Amen."

PART ONE . . . PREPARATION

"We, Thy children, close the door of the outer world." Sit down quietly and turn your attention to the kingdom of heaven which Jesus tells us is within. We close the door by thinking of spiritual instead of material things.

"And contemplate Thy holy presence." We become like the thing upon which we fix our thoughts. To bring forth the Christ, we must think as He does.

PART TWO . . . RECEPTION

"We feel the Christ love flowing through us. All that is unlike Thee disappears." Picture this love as a great white, sparkling light flooding your entire being. It is NOW washing away all weakness and all limitation, leaving you pure, holy and healed.

"We are filled with Thy purifying love which supplies our spiritual and our physical needs." When you repeat these words, beloved, feel in the depths of your heart that the love of Christ does now fill your every need.

PART THREE . . . DISTRIBUTION

"We radiate this love to all the world to bless Thy
children everywhere." The law of life is ebb and flow,
receive and give out. We have received and we are filled
with the healing love of Christ. Now it is our joy to gladly
pass that blessing on to others. One should keep a list of
names for healing prayers and at this point, should read
the names aloud if possible. Send a blessing out every day
to the entire world. You are a radiating center of divine
love, a channel through which the healing love of Christ is
being sent to His beloved children.

PART FOUR . . . THANKSGIVING

"We give thanks that we have received. The word has
gone forth to bless and to heal in the Name of the living
Christ . . . Amen." Jesus always prayed the affirmative
prayer, such as "Father, I thank Thee that Thou hast
heard me." (John 11:4) Praise and gratitude have a power
of increase. In blessing others you have received a blessing
and your part of the work is finished, for you hold God by
His own divine law which cannot be broken.

In our next lesson a special prayer for protection will be
given. This prayer never fails to protect God's children
from all danger.

"And the prayer of faith shall save the sick." (James
5:15)

Peace be with you.

Questions on Daily Lesson Nine

1. *Does divine revelation belong to any special race?*
2. *What does the number four mean in the Bible?*
3. *How must we prepare for prayer?*
4. *How should we picture this love?*
5. *What law are we using in this prayer?*
6. *What does "blessing" do for us?*
7. *When we have prepared, received, given out, and thanked, is there more to be done?*

The Protection of the Christ

Beloved, this is a most important lesson. Your Lord Jesus Christ has not left you unprotected amid the dangers of the outer world through which you are traveling. Commit to memory the laws of protection. Give them to others freely for it is the will of the Christ that His beloved shall be protected. "Even there shall Thy hand lead me and Thy right hand shall hold me." (Ps. 139:10)

THE STATEMENT

My help cometh from the Lord, which made
heaven and earth.   *Psalm 91*

With the coming of Christ to this earth His own holy name was given to us for our use. "Hitherto ye have asked nothing in my name; ask and ye shall receive that your joy may be full." (John 16:24) We have failed to accept the promise of divine protection that is given in the words "For there is none other name under heaven given among men, whereby we must be saved." (Acts 4:12) From what is man to be saved? Only sin? Has the promise of God a boundary? No, beloved, when you call on this holy name, you are saved not only from sin but from all evil and

52

danger and even from the fear of these things. "Thou shalt not be afraid for the terror by night." (Ps. 91:5)

Three separate protections are given in this lesson and one should use all three daily. The first is the Wall of Fire (see Zec. 2:5). The second is the Auric Cleansing (see 2nd Cor. 7:1) and the third is the Armour of Light found in Eph. 6:11-18.

The first protection consists of a very simple but positive statement that can be said silently or aloud. "I build a wall of living flame around me in the Name of Jesus Christ." All of these protection statements should be memorized.

The second protection is the cleansing and recharging of your aura which becomes contaminated by negative thoughts, either your own or others. "In the Name, through the Power and by the Word of Jesus Christ, my aura is cleansed of everything but the pure white light of the Christ. My aura is recharged with the same white light of the Christ."

The third protection is the greatest and most powerful of them all. It is an individual protection for all teachers, healers and spiritual workers. When seen by the extended vision, it is a dazzling, sparkling white. You clothe yourself in this armour by a positive statement condensed from the Bible verses. It can be said silently or aloud. "In the Name, through the Power and by the Word of Christ Jesus, I put on the whole Armour of Light. On my head is the helmet of Salvation. I wear the breastplate of Righteousness. My loins are girded with the Truth. My feet are shod with Peace and enveloped in the flame of the spirit of Almighty God. In my left hand I hold the shield of Faith. In my right hand is the sword of the Spirit. This is the Word of God and the Word of God is unassailable. Only Good shall come to me.

"Thus clad, I stand joyfully expectant, ready to do the Will of the Father.   Amen."

Use any or all of these protections every day, especially
before arising and retiring. Because this protection is of
such high radiation, it does not last long and has to be
renewed at least every eight hours. When needed,
however, it is instantaneous and you are absolutely protected mentally, physically and spiritually.

Protect yourself before entering the Silence. Also protect those who may be with you and those for whom you
pray. Protect again AFTER your spiritual work is completed. In the Silence you enter the subjective realm where
you are open and receptive; you have to be or you could
not receive. In this realm, you use up your forces even
your protection, and that is why it has to be renewed when
the work is finished.

The power of all these protections lies in the use of the
holy Name of Christ. "The name of the Lord is a strong
tower; the righteous runneth into it and is safe." (Prov.
18:10)

Peace be with you.

Questions on Daily Lesson Ten

1. *Is man always promised protection?*
2. *Whose name is given for our protection?*
3. *Is this protection limited?*
4. *Describe the Wall of Flame.*
5. *Why is it necessary to cleanse your aura?*
6. *Describe the Armour of Light.*
7. *Why does this protection have to be renewed?*

Making Protection Practical

We already use the power of protection every moment of every day and night, consciously or unconsciously. When we dress in the morning, we protect ourselves from the heat or cold, the rain or the sun. When we eat, we guard against consuming too much or too little; against too many or too few carbohydrates or proteins.

We take care when we choose friends, for we avoid those who irritate us or who would treat us wrongly. We protect our minds by stimulation and relaxation. We guard ourselves at night when we pray our prayers of protection.

When we do not consciously or subconsciously apply the rules of protection which serve as checks and balances in our lives, we react in body, mind and/or spirit. We are ill or sad.

The prayers of protection which we are learning in these lessons offer spiritual guards which operate on all planes of our existence. They come from the very heart of our Creator. These particular prayers have stood the test of time since they were given to Mrs. Thedick more than fifty years ago and are used daily by thousands of people.

Their continued use adds strength and vitality to their power. Every sincere prayer rises to our Creative Force from which we stem. Sustained use of any prayer gives impetus to the stream of prayer going heavenward. This is true of our prayers of protection and also of the Lord's Prayer with which we close our meditational time. The Lord's Prayer is such a part of our devotional pattern all over the world that there is a constant stream of power present from its use.

Some may retreat from asking for protection through prayer, insisting they are automatically protected by the Lord, and it is true that His protection is always where we are. So are our clothes when we get up in the morning but we must put them on to be protected from the weather. So is our food, but we must eat to be protected from hunger and weakness.

Thus it is with protection. Prayers of protection are a high vibration of light, generally unseen, but of such high velocity and power that anything unlike our special pattern cannot penetrate. Like any high energy, however, the light dissipates unless renewed through continued contact with Creative Source. Our asking for the light to be around us is the necessary contact.

Some may also shy away from asking that the Light of the Christ be around them lest experiences they desire also be kept away. "I don't want to be in a shell," they say. "I'll just take my chances," they insist.

A coat keeps the chill of the air from freezing us or making us uncomfortable. It doesn't keep the air itself away from us so that we cannot breathe. Prayers of protection fend off what is not part of our divine pattern, never that which is right for us.

Strong emotions such as fear or anger quickly use up the vibrations of protective prayer. It is good to form the habit of quickly building a Wall of Flame around yourself whenever there is extra tension. The prayers are also especially helpful at times of illness or surgery, or when there is an accident.

The Light of the Christ may be put around others at any time as well as one's self. Almost instinctively we know we should not intrude into the depths of another without their permission, but the Light of Christ surrounding them can never be an intrusive factor. You may find asking that a Wall of Flame be built around someone who is an undesirable factor in your life can be very helpful. It may be such a help to them that you actually benefit.

Learn the prayers of protection "by heart", not "by rote." They can become such a part of you that you see the Light of God around yourself, your dear ones, even situations you are facing when you first open your eyes in the morning. Let this become a habit of the heart, not merely the mind.

Renew the protection at your especial low time of the day . . . noontime . . . mid-afternoon . . . you know your own need. Turn yourself and your loved ones over to Creative Force of the Christ at your time of sleep and know that all is well.

The Christ Light

Beloved, always remember that you are children of the light . . . "the true light that lighteth every man that cometh into the world." (John 1:9) This knowledge is of little use to you unless you use it. Daily recognize your divine inheritance as children of the light. "I am the Light of the world," Jesus said in John 8:12. "Ye are the light of the world," He told us in Matt. 5:14. These words of His are just as true today as when He spoke them. Never forget that "your Father is the Father of light, in whom there is no shadow of turning."

You are his beloved child.

THE STATEMENT

The Lord is my light.   *John 1:1-14*

In our spiritual studies we find that the foundation of all things is expressed in the Trinity, Father, Son and Holy Spirit, of love, life and light. The Father is love, "God so loved the world that He gave His only begotten Son." (John 3:16) The Son is life, "I am come that they might

have life and that they might have it more abundantly."
(John 10:10) The Holy Spirit is light. "Know ye not that
ye are the temple of God and that the Spirit of God
dwelleth in you." (I Cor. 3:16)

We have been taught so little about being children of
light, sons and daughters of the living God. We have
almost forgotten our real nature and our Lord's command, "let your light shine." (Matt. 5:16) Notice, beloved, the word is LET your light shine. You already have
this light within you. You were born with it and you
brought it with you into this school of experience. It is
your passport and your identification papers. Beloved,
you are indeed a child of light. A light-bringer! A light-
bearer come to "give light to them that sit in darkness."
(Luke 1:79)

The loving Lord never desired that you should stumble
along in the dark, so He placed a spark of His divine light
within you when He called you into being. When the
Father who is love sent you forth, He gave you life which
is the Son and from life comes light, which is the Holy
Spirit.

You may ask, "Where is this Holy Spirit?" Deep within
the heart of your being is a holy place, a sanctuary, and
there upon an altar burns the light of the Holy Spirit. We
place before this altar the veils of selfishness, vanity, fear
and other negative thoughts, until the light of the Holy
Spirit within us shines dimmer and dimmer.

We are told, "Quench not the Spirit." (I Thes. 5:19) We
must remove the veils and "LET THE LIGHT SHINE."
This is very easy, beloved, but because of its simplicity, it
has eluded us. Listen! The Son, who is life, gives us light.
We must keep that light burning brightly so it can pierce
through the veil. To do this, we need the first part of the
Trinity, which is the Father or love.

You are a small universe, a duplicate of the greater

Universe which is composed of love, life and light. You
must enter the sanctuary within your own heart and feed
the flame of light burning upon the altar there with the oil
of divine love. "Then shall thy light break forth as the
morning . . . and the glory of the Lord shall be thy
reward." (Isa. 58:8)

Peace be with you.

QUESTIONS ON DAILY LESSON ELEVEN

1. What is the foundation of Creation represented by?
2. Explain Father, Son and Holy Spirit.
3. What is your passport?
4. Where is the Holy Spirit?
5. Describe the sanctuary.
6. What dims the light within?
7. What must we do to keep the flame burning?

The Christ Consciousness

Beloved, do you realize that you have studied eleven lessons already? This lesson completes the first step to the "Temple of Light." The next lesson will start you on the second step to that temple. Have these lessons made you happier, healthier, more at peace? Is that precious blossom, the "Christ Consciousness," blooming in the garden of your heart? We rejoice with you to see that blossom appear. We know that this greatly desired, sought after and prayed for state, the Christ Consciousness is now coming forth in you.

THE STATEMENT

In Him I live and move and have my being.
Acts 17:23–32

The dictionary defines consciousness as direct knowledge. These twelve lessons have been given to you that you might receive direct knowledge of Christ. There were certain steps necessary to take to attain this end. The Master of love has taught you through these lessons how to plant the little seed. You must water it with faith, cultivate it with hope, and bring forth the rose of divine love as well as the flowers of forgiveness, peace, prayer, protection and illumination.

Your heart's garden is now a holy place, "where the Lord can walk in the cool of the day." (Gen. 3:8) He gives to you His Consciousness or direct knowledge of Him. Beloved seeker of truth, no special food, exercise, teacher or study can ever give *this* to you. Peace, forgiveness, faith and love must be lived daily.

Always seek His face in prayer. Recognize only One Power and One Presence, your Lord, Jesus Christ. Do not seek in the outer that which the loving Christ is waiting to give you, Himself. These lessons are meant only to point the way to reach the goal . . . Christ Consciousness.

To be Christ-Conscious is to have the thought of Christ uppermost in your mind. You often hear the term, "air-minded" and you know it means thinking a great deal about aviation. When we become Christ-Conscious or "Christ-minded", then our hearts and minds are full of love for Jesus Christ.

We do not become Christ-Conscious all at once. We gradually unfold in consciousness, becoming that to which we give our greatest attention. For instance, you may have a partial unfoldment of this consciousness along the line of health. You may realize the Christ Consciousness as your perfect health.

Beloved, it is more than health of body. It is the kingdom of heaven or harmony on all planes of action, including mental, physical and spiritual. Jesus Christ Himself is the way . . . the Christ Highway. He told us plainly, "I am the way, the truth and the life, and no man cometh unto the Father but by me. (John 14:6) In the Bible the rules of life are laid down. Everything we need to know is written there, but it is necessary to be, "doers of the word and not hearers only." (James 1:22)

To be doers, you must dedicate yourself and all you have to Him. Listen to His voice in the Silence. Place yourself and all your affairs lovingly in His hands. "And ye shall seek me and find me, when ye shall search for me with all your heart." (Jer. 29:13)

This Christ Consciousness, beloved, MUST BE LIVED EACH DAY. "But as many as received Him, to them He gave power to become the Sons of God, even to them that believe on His Name." (John 1:12)

Peace be with you.

QUESTIONS ON DAILY LESSON TWELVE

1. *What is consciousness?*
2. *Can the Christ Consciousness come from without?*
3. *How can we live it?*
4. *Is it possible to have a partial unfoldment of the Christ Consciousness?*
5. *Is this Consciousness quickly unfolded?*
6. *Where are the rules of life found?*
7. *Why must we seek with all our heart?*

Unfolding Your Own Pattern

Beloved, we have completed the first twelve lessons which show the first step to the Temple of Light. We became conscious of our Holy Lord Christ and then we tried to be like Him. In the study of these lessons, the seed was sown and it grew and blossomed.

Here at the conclusion of the section is a good time to pause and evaluate how much you have enlarged your knowledge of the Christ Consciousness, for these first twelve lessons were first printed as a separate unit with no realization that there would be more.

Eleanore Thedick, the very aware individual who wrote down these messages, always wore an apron except on very "dress-up" occasions. She kept a notebook and pencil in the pocket. She was given a clear mental picture that the thought of Christ must be uppermost in our minds and hearts to attain Christ Consciousness. She put that idea into words along with the other image of the heart's garden being a place in which to plant the seeds of Christ qualities one would like to have bloom.

Gradually, one by one, the other eleven lessons were given; she noted them and all went into the apron pocket. Not that her learning stayed there, for she always shared her guidance, especially with a small group who met in her home on a regular basis. The lessons developed into a course which she taught and eventually into a pamphlet

which the group published. This was during the years of
the Depression and the class held bake sales to finance
the printing.

"The lessons were given to me to share," Mrs. Thedick
said. "They are warmly loving, but impersonal and they
follow the plan of God's law and order.

"Our God does not change His laws for individuals. His
law and order are much more vast than we know. If we
think we have a miracle, for instance, we are only tapping
into a law of God that we haven't known about. We can
learn the laws; let them be fulfilled in our lives, and then
we will have divine order."

The first twelve lessons are signposts, just as the Bible is
a signpost. To study either or both, is to get a deeper
understanding that Christ Jesus is also within us as the
Christ Consciousness, the image and likeness of God.
That same Spirit is outside us as teacher and friend. The
Christ assumed a body of flesh as Jesus, the man, and
went through the human conditions and experiences that
we do, conquering all. Using that same Spirit, we may also
conquer. We will be able to more fully understand the
intricacies of the code in which the Holy Bible is written.

The experiences we are having are part of our Christ
Highway. Take time now to see how far you have traveled
on your special road.

Follow the routine you have established.

Check that your protection is good; your aura cleansed
of everything but the pure white light of the Christ and
that you have on the whole armour of light.

Invite in those heavenly helpers whom you would like to
work with you. Your guardian angel surely will be asked,
as will the Angels of Protection and the Angels of Beauty
and Balance with whom we have become familiar.
Perhaps you would like to invite the Angel Gabriel to be
with you for Gabriel represents love and you would like
to evidence this quality. The healing angel, Raphael, is

available as is the Angel Azrael, who cares for you at the time of your birth into this world as well as your birth into your next experience.

Be still.

Listen.

What other angels cross your mind as possible companions for this experience? Invite those who seem to fit into the expression you intend to bring forth. Would it be Angels of Peace? Of Music? Of Perfume? Perfume is the breath of God. Of Prosperity? Or Government? Angels of Children will be glad to come, as will Angels of the Family. Nature Angels are anxious to help. Angels of Education are nearby if you call for them. You will know your need and recognize their presence.

Invite them to be present and to share with you. Speak to them as though they were in the room with you, for they are. Give them the opportunity to help the Christ by sharing with you, just as you enjoy yourself, sharing with others. It is thus when you allow the angels to widen your horizons that they fulfill their reason for existence. In the Bible, the word angel means a messenger or bringer of tidings, we are told in Cruden's Unabridged Concordance, March 1973, page 10.

Speak to the angels.

Speak also to the Christ, for the Christ Consciousness is always with you.

Listen to the angels.

Listen to the Christ. Discover how much you have matured in your perceptions.

Only you can know where you were, where you are and where you are going; but you can know and you can grow. This you are doing if you are studying, listening, experimenting and accepting answers along the Christ Highway.

After your communion with the Lord and the angels, allow a time of quietness. Keep a listening ear and a willing heart. Be available for any special truth to unfold to you.

Experience a feeling of sweetness.

Feel the lightness of spirit which the unfolding of beauty and balance brings to your life.

Know that your own pattern will unfold ever more clearly every day, for your quiet time turns your personal will over to the divine will of Creative Force.

Relish the joy that wells up within you.

Give thanks.

Renew the pure white light of the Christ around you and be sure your feet are planted on solid ground.

Pray the Lord's Prayer.

Begin the study of the next twelve lessons.

The Christ Quality . . . Faith

Beloved, you are now standing upon the second step to the Temple. This step is called the Christ Qualities, or the Fruit of the Tree of Life. This fruit or these qualities comes forth in body, mind and affairs. Day by day as we study, meditate and pray, we "eat" of the fruit, thus assimilating and building these Christ qualities into our being. This is the "tree of life that bears twelve manner of fruits." (Rev. 22:2)

THE STATEMENT

Lord, I believe . . . help Thou my unbelief.

Luke 7:1-10

Let us review Daily Lesson Two where we see something wonderful taking place; where a great law is in operation. As seekers for light, we desire to know more about this marvelous principle called "faith." We find there are three steps necessary to bring forth faith in its fullest expression.

First - Desire: This is the first step in bringing forth the great law of Faith. We wish or desire that our loved ones

68

or ourselves be healed of sickness or limitation. The natural law of life is health and abundance of all good. It is natural to desire to be well and free from lack. That deep desire within your heart for all good of whatever nature is the flaming light of Faith that never goes out.

Second - Obedience: Most people do not get beyond the first step of desiring or wishing for things to be better. They pray, "oh, please God, hear and answer my prayer: make things better." To make things better, beloved, we must take the second step - Obedience. Our prayer must be, "show me Thy will."

We learn by carefully reading our Bibles and seeing what Jesus did. All who went to Jesus for healing had to show their faith by some simple act of obedience. Read Matt. 12:13, Luke 17:14, John 5:8 and John 9:7. This same law was used by the prophets of long ago for healing. (see Kings 5:10) Jesus Christ used different methods to heal but all were based on faith in Him. He often said, "according to thy faith be it unto you." (Matt. 9:29)

Third - Action: This is the last step in bringing forth the light of Faith from within. Jesus gave many commands to the needy ones, "Stretch forth thy hand;" (Matt. 12:13) "Show thyself to the priests;" (Luke 17:14) "Take up thy bed and walk" (Matt. 9:6) and many others, all illustrating active faith.

Beloved, you say, "but He is not here today, walking the streets and healing the sick." The same Jesus is here now, right in your midst. You reach Him through your consciousness. With the study of these lessons and your faith, you have been building the Christ Consciousness that you and your Lord may be united. This is your test of Faith.

If you wish healing or freedom from any limitation, go and sit quietly alone and turn your attention to the Great Healer, Jesus Christ, your friend and brother. Make your requests known to Him with thanksgiving. Pray the prayer of Obedience. Say, "What must I do? Not my will, but Thy will be mine."

You will receive that which you seek according to your faith as you wait upon your Lord in the secret place within your own heart.

"Ask and it shall be given you; seek and ye shall find." (Luke 11:9)

Peace be with you.

QUESTIONS ON DAILY LESSON THIRTEEN

1. *What is the first step to the Temple of Light?*
2. *What is the second step?*
3. *Describe the three steps that underlie the law of Faith.*
4. *What have you been building through the study of these lessons?*
5. *How do you reach Christ for healing?*
6. *What is the prayer of obedience?*
7. *Why is it necessary to ask?*

The Christ Quality . . . Strength

Beloved, these lessons are not given to you to increase your knowledge of metaphysical subjects. They build a bridge for you over which you can reach your teacher and friend, Jesus Christ. These lessons are the links in a golden chain of love of which your Lord is the beginning and the end. "I am Alpha and Omega, the beginning and the ending." (Rev. 1:8)

THE STATEMENT

In quietness and confidence is my strength.

Ps. 46:1–11

Today more than any time in the history of the world we need to cultivate the Christ quality of Strength. We see the old prophecies fulfilled before our eyes and a great spirit of unrest is everywhere present. We, the children of light, become more confident and quiet as the noise and confusion increases about us. We know from whom our strength comes. "The Lord is the strength of my life; of whom shall I be afraid?" (Ps. 27:1) We are poised, calm, peaceful, unhurried and confident of the outcome of events.

71

When we live in the personal consciousness, we are fear-
ful, doubtful, wavering and uncertain as to what to do or
what road to follow. Many voices call to us. "And they
shall say to you, see here or see there; go not after them
nor follow them." (Luke 17:23) If we listen, we lose our
way for there is but one Way—the Christ Way. Our very
uncertainty prevents our demonstration or overcoming, as
it is called in the Bible. The mind of man is like a lake and
only when it is calm and peaceful can it mirror perfection.

The Christ quality of Strength, like Faith, is a trinity. It
is composed of three parts, not steps, as in the case of
Faith. These three parts, when combined, bring forth
Strength on all planes, physical, mental and spiritual.
Hence, beloved, let us plan carefully, for we desire to
bring forth into the outer expression of life the Strength of
the Christ.

Loyalty is first in the trinity of Strength. To be loyal to
Christ means that He and He alone must be first in your
life. When we are loyal to any cause, we give that cause
our physical, mental and spiritual support. "No man can
serve two masters." (Matt. 6:24) No human being has the
right to judge the depth of your loyality to Christ for
that is sacred between you and your Lord.

Courage is second in the trinity of Strength. When we
are "strong in the Lord," (Eph. 6.10) then we are
courageous, fearless and unafraid. Many are the promises
of renewed courage and strength all through the Bible. If
you lack courage, beloved, read Psalms 27:1, Isa. 25:4 and
Isa. 41:10. Personal courage will never sustain you in your
hour of need. You have a spiritual courage that is your
divine birthright.

As you become conscious of the everlasting arms of
love, your courage never falters. "The eternal God is thy
refuge and underneath are the everlasting arms." (Deut.
33:27) You can meet all difficulties and do all things
through the power of this Indwelling One.

Endurance is third in the trinity of Strength. To endure is to be patient and to keep on trying never to admit defeat. Always remember that Strength is a trinity composed of Loyalty, Courage and Endurance. "But he that shall endure unto the end, the same shall be saved." (Matt. 23:13)

First . . . Loyalty to Christ; giving your Lord the first place in your life. "And ye shall seek Me and find Me when ye shall search for Me with all thy heart." (Jer. 10:27)

Second . . . the Courage to follow where He heads, "My sheep hear My voice and I know them and they follow Me." (John 10:27)

Third . . . the Endurance and patience that recognizes no failures. That place where we can say with Paul, "This one thing I do, forgetting those things which are behind and reaching forth into those things which are before, I press toward the mark, for the price of the high calling of God in Christ Jesus." (Phil. 3:13-14)

Peace be with you.

QUESTIONS ON DAILY LESSON FOURTEEN

1. *As children of light, what is our attitude?*
2. *What is the One Way?*
3. *How does Faith resemble Strength?*
4. *What comes first in the trinity of Strength?*
5. *What is second?*
6. *What is third in the trinity?*
7. *Explain the meaning of Endurance.*

The Christ Quality . . . Wisdom

Beloved, as you "eat" of the fruit of Faith and Strength of the Tree of Life, you incorporate these Christ qualities into your own being. Faith and Strength bring forth Wisdom or Judgment. This is the perfect trinity, the underlying principle of all creation. Wisdom is the key which will unlock all doors to you. Eat freely of this fruit.

THE STATEMENT

I have a wise and understanding heart.

Prov. 2:1–10

In this lesson we learn more about the "eyes" of Faith, for Faith has two eyes, Wisdom and Understanding. If we do not use these two qualities, Faith is blind. "He that lacketh these things is blind." (2 Peter 1:9) When we understand anything, we always say, "I see," meaning we perceive or understand. When our Wisdom and Understanding are illumined by the light of Christ, then our eyes of Faith are open and we see the hidden truths. We *know* just what to do and the door of revelation stands open before us.

In the Bible there are two kinds of wisdom mentioned.

There is the wisdom of God and the wisdom of men. "For the wisdom of this world is foolishness with God." (1 Cor. 3:19) The wisdom of God is called "the wisdom from above." (James 3:17) It is intuition or Inner Teachings. One has a great desire, when wisdom is unfolding, to read the Book of Life that God spreads out before us. "Ask the beasts and they shall teach thee." (Job 12:7)

Our Lord bade us seek that we might find. To find the wisdom of God, we must seek with humility. We must be receptive and willing to learn. Beloved, if you let pride into your heart, wisdom is shut out. Pride belongs to the wisdom of man, not the wisdom of God. It blinds the "eyes of Faith," causing the feet to stumble. The Bible is full of incidents recording the downfall of great souls through pride. "For all that is in the world, the lust of the flesh, the lust of the eyes and the pride of life, is not of the Father, but is of the world." (1 John 2:16)

Wisdom is symbolized by a beautiful temple. We wish to enter, but before we can walk in the "Courts of Wisdom," we must pass through three gates. Over the first gate is written "Humility." To receive the wisdom of God, we must be very humble. One of the principles of humility is the willingness to listen. Our Lord speaks, but we drown His voice in our clamor for gifts. To pass the first gate, our prayer must be, "Show me Thy ways, Oh, Lord. Teach me Thy paths." (Ps. 25:4)

The tiny bird and the mighty ocean each have a message for us if we will but listen humbly to them. All nature sings a song of joyous praise to the Creator. Turn the pages of the Book of Life reverently and be "just a little child." As we willingly sit at the feet of the Christ and learn of Him, then we are ready to pass through the gate of Humility.

"The mouth of the righteous speaketh wisdom and his tongue talketh of judgment." (Ps. 37:30)

Peace be with you.

QUESTIONS ON DAILY LESSON FIFTEEN

1. *What key unlocks all doors?*
2. *Describe the "eyes of Faith."*
3. *Name two kinds of wisdom mentioned in the Bible.*
4. *Give another name for intuition.*
5. *What blinds the "eyes of Faith?"*
6. *What must we do before we can enter the Temple of Wisdom?*
7. *Give the name of the first gate.*

The Christ Quality . . .
Understanding

Beloved, with all thy getting get understanding. While studying these lessons on Wisdom and Understanding, pray the affirmative prayer. Rejoice and give thanks that your "eyes of Faith" are open and the deep things of God are made clear to you.

THE STATEMENT

My eyes of Faith are open. I see clearly and understand.
Job 28:12–28

It looks very easy to "eat" of the fruit of Wisdom and Understanding, but there is a great deal more than appears on the surface. In the last lesson, Wisdom was spoken of as a beautiful temple. We longed to enter, but found that there were three gates through which to pass. Over the first gate was written, "Humility." We learned how to pass through that gate. Now we stand before the second gate and the name above it is "Patience."

In our great desire for Wisdom and Understanding, we

77

often get impatient. Our spiritual progress seems so very slow. Beloved, many make the mistake here of trying to hurry or force spiritual unfoldment. It is possible to bring out a forced spiritual growth by putting forth much activity. Like the hothouse flower, this forced growth has no depth and it soon fades away.

It is very necessary to be patient, not only with others, but also with ourselves. To know that the greater the expression, the longer it takes to come forth in the objective world, is to know patience. We must not only be humble, but patient, if we wish to walk in the "courts of Wisdom." Sometimes we have to wait a long time outside the gate called "Patience." Wait till all anxiety, all resistance, all impatience has given place to peace. "Then through faith and patience we inherit the promises." (Heb. 6:12)

As soon as we are ready to say, "Thy way, Lord, not my way," then we find that we have passed the portal of Patience. Now we are standing before the last gate which is called Service, but this is not a difficult gate to go through. Humility and Patience bring forth a great desire to serve others.

In our new, humble state of mind, we see no one as great or small, wise or foolish, but all as children of the One Father, "Who is above all and through all and in you all." (Eph. 4:6) As we gladly serve, "in His Name," we eat the fruit of Wisdom and Understanding and enter the Temple.

"Therefore get wisdom and with all thy getting, get understanding." (Prov. 4:7)

Peace be with you.

Questions on Daily Lesson Sixteen

1. *What symbol is used to describe Wisdom?*
2. *What must we pass through before we can enter the temple?*
3. *What is the name of the first gate?*
4. *Name the second gate.*
5. *Name the third gate.*
6. *What is the result of forcing spiritual unfoldment?*
7. *What does the union of Patience and Humility bring forth?*

Giving Thanks

In Daily Lesson Sixteen we are taught to pray the affirmative prayer; to rejoice and give thanks rather than continuing to petition and ask for answers. Nowhere is this more beneficial than in seeking the Christ quality of Patience in our lives.

Patience is listed as one of the two gates through which we must pass to get Understanding. If we constantly ask God to give us patience, there is no way for this to come about other than working through experiences where our patience seems to be required. This is one way to learn the quality of Patience, but not the only one. The way of experience is often painful.

How much easier, then, to thank God that you are already patient. Rejoice that you can accept patience as part of you, rather than suffering to learn lessons. Be willing to accept that the yoke of the Christ is really easy. (Matt. 11:30) Claim patience. Give thanks for it. Know it is one of your attributes. Show it in your life.

Walk through the gates marked Humility and Patience and get Understanding easily, giving thanks.

If you cannot accept this with your mind; if it seems difficult to feel that giving thanks for a quality can make it appear in your thoughts and actions, go once more into a meditational time.

You will remember how to do this, first putting on the whole armour of light so that you are protected and grounded.

Then, you will delight to invite the Lord Christ and your special angels to be with you. You will want to include the Angels of Humility and Patience this time so that they may communicate with you.

Each time you meditate you are more and more able to assume an attitude of communion with the Christ of your inner self. At this moment, ask that Christ to fill you with the assurance of Humility and Patience as already being part of you.

Listen as the Angels of Humility and the Angels of Patience let you know of the joy of expressing these qualities. Feel yourself become large with the sweetness of these attributes. You are overwhelmed and become still, breathing in the Understanding which results. You inhale and receive and exhale and send out these same qualities into the atmosphere for others to pick up.

Slowly you know that you are securely patient and humble. You understand and you give thanks to God for His gifts to you.

Quietly you renew your protective prayer garb and get ready to resume your daily activities.

You are now willing and able to be humble in the finest sense as you know yourself to be a clear channel through which the Christ can work. You do not need personal gratification, nor do you need to take a lowly place. You are secure. You learn more of the Christ within from the Christ without.

You give thanks for a calm, serene life, knowing you are patient. You are untroubled by the inconveniences and disturbances around you. You do not need to work out a large amount of emotions. You accept that the Way of the Lord will shine through to you.

You are already patient . . . joyously so!

The repetition of the Lord's Prayer swells to a larger proportion as it joins the enternal chorus of prayer going heavenward and you are grateful for another time apart.

The Christ Quality . . . Love

INSTRUCTION TO THE SEEKER: DAILY LESSON SEVENTEEN

Beloved, if you desire more health, peace or good of any nature, then love more, for Love is another name for God. During the study of this lesson as you "eat" of the fruit of Love, think the loving thought and do the loving act. Look for something lovable in everyone you meet. "By this shall men know that ye are my disciples, if ye have love one to another." (John 13:35)

THE STATEMENT

I love my Lord and keep His commandments.

John 15:1-17

In First Corinthians (Chapter 13) is found one of the greatest treatises on love ever written. Study it and use the "wisdom key" to unlock the door to the mysteries of God. "Unto you it is given to know the mystery of the kingdom of God." (Mark 4:11) Never has there been a time and never will there be a time when Love is not with us. We come into this expression of life with it and when we leave this life for a greater one, Love is still our companion. We cannot destroy Love. We can veil it, imprison it, cast it aside, forget it, but because it is one of the principles of the great Trinity it is indestructible.

The first great principle is Love. "Beloved, let us love one another for love is of God." (1 John 4:7) As we love one another we fulfill the law of God for God is Love. "No man hath seen God at any time. If we love one another, God dwelleth in us." (1 John 4:12)

The second great principle is Life. "In Him was Life and the Life was the Light of men." (John 1:4) "I am come that they might have Life and that they might have it more abundantly." (John 10:10) Our life is hid in Christ. We have no life apart from Him.

The third great principle is Light. Christ was the "true Light that lighteth every man that cometh into the world." (John 1:9) If we try to walk the path of life by our own light, we walk in darkness. "And the Light shineth in darkness and the darkness comprehendeth it not." (John 1:5) Jesus said, "I am the Light of the world; he that followeth me shall not walk in darkness but shall have the Light of life." (John 8:12)

On this great Trinity of Love, Life and Light rests the foundation of all things created. "All things were made by Him and without Him was not anything made that was made." (John 1:3) Man is a miniature universe and he builds his world about him according to his understanding and his use of these three principles. If he lacks Light, his world is a dark one; if he lacks Love, then it is cold and unfriendly. If he expresses Life only from the selfish plane, it brings him sorrow.

How necessary that we as co-creators who are made in the Image of God should learn to work harmoniously with the great laws and principles of creation. We have a perfect example set before us. Let us follow in His steps. The way is plain and the banner over us is Love.

"If ye love Me, keep my commandments." (John 14:15)

Peace be with you.

QUESTIONS ON DAILY LESSON SEVENTEEN

1. *How can you attract more good into your life?*
2. *Why is Love indestructible?*
3. *Give the name and the nature of the first principle.*
4. *Name and nature of second.*
5. *Name and nature of third.*
6. *How does man build his world?*
7. *Who is our leader and what is his banner?*

The Christ Quality . . . Power

Beloved, this fruit of power *must* be eaten with wisdom and understanding. Many ships on the sea of life have been wrecked on the rock of personal power. Let us remember that only in the Temple of Wisdom is found the real and lasting power . . . God Power.

THE STATEMENT

God is the only power and the only presence.

Ps. 62:1–13

Beloved seeker of Light, you have reached the second cycle in your study of the Christ Consciousness. To divide these thirty-six lessons into four cycles of nine lessons each is necessary to build your "city foursquare" spoken of in Rev. 21:16.

Let us review a little. In Daily Lessons 2, 8, 12, 14, 15 and 17, three steps or parts are mentioned. In Lesson 9, four parts or steps are explained. Creation or the Godhead rests on a three-fold foundation but manifests through a four-fold expression. If you desire a deeper understanding of this, meditate on Daily Lesson 17.

Our lesson today is on Power and there is but one
Power, just as there is but one Life and one God. "The
Father, of whom are all things and we in Him, and one
Lord Jesus Christ by whom are all things, and we by
Him." (1 Cor. 8:6) Nevertheless, man has free will and he
can use this Power as he desires. To understand the effect
of Power in the life of the individual, we divide it into
three parts.

First . . . physical power. To glory in our physical efforts and to rejoice in our ability to use earthly power is to
cut ourselves off from our Source. The possession of the
things of this earth gained through physical or earthly
power never brings lasting satisfaction for, "the flesh pro-
fiteth nothing." (John 6:63) Acknowledge God, beloved,
as the only power in your body and in your affairs.

Second . . . mental power. When we depend on the
power of our minds and try to conquer by our mental
power, we fight a losing battle. "There is no power but of
God: the powers that be are ordained of God." (Rom.
13:1) To conquer the mental realm, "Let this mind be in
you which was also in Christ Jesus." (Phil. 2:5) Follow
His steps and use His method for He did all His works by
depending on the Power within, which He named Father.
It was not until He had finished His mission and had overcome even death that He said, "All power is given unto
Me in heaven and in earth." (Matt. 28:18)

Third . . . spiritual power or heavenly power. This is
God-given power, according to St. Paul who says in II
Cor. 13:10 "Therefore I write these things . . . according
to the power which the Lord hath given me . . . " If
spiritual power is used in a physical or mental way, its
possibilities are limited.

All three of these powers are God-power. As we recognize
the truth that all manifestations of power, physical, mental and spiritual are one and the same, namely God-power,
so we develop harmoniously.

"For the kingdom of God is not in word, but in power." (Cor. 4:20)

Peace be with you.

Questions on Daily Lesson Eighteen

1. *Where is real Power found?*
2. *Explain the Trinity and its manifestations.*
3. *What is the difference between physical, mental and spiritual power?*
4. *Can we limit power?*
5. *How can we conquer the mental realm?*
6. *What did Jesus name this power within?*
7. *What is the result of a recognition that all power is is God-power?*

The Christ Quality
. . . Imagination

Beloved, eat slowly of the fruits of the Tree of Life. This is the time to read over the last six lessons and ask yourself these questions: "how much Faith, Wisdom, Strength, Understanding, Love and Power have I built into my consciousness? Am I growing more Christlike daily? Am I following my Lord all the way?"

THE STATEMENT

I am made in His Image.

Gen. 1:24–31

One of the greatest mysteries of the Bible is found in Gen. 1:27 which tells of the creation of man in the Image of his God. Much has been written on this subject but a very vital point is overlooked. The word Image means a representation of some person or thing. Beloved, *you* are a representation of God Almighty sent to this earth as His agent, sign or symbol, to carry out His divine plans. You create as He creates, by thought, but God's creations are perfect. "And God saw everything He had made, and behold, it was very good." (Gen. 1:31) Man being in a state of unfolding consciousness creates according to his finite understanding.

There is but one way for man to create perfectly and that is by letting the mind of Christ be in him. When we *let* this mind be in us, then we bring forth the Christ Quality of Imagination. The positive aspect of Imaginaton is sometimes called vision, while its negative aspect is sometimes called desire. It is very necessary that we cultivate the positive aspect. Be open and receptive toward the Lord. Should your revelation come in the form of a vision, then ask for the interpretation. Read Job's explanation of a vision. (Job 33:14–17)

All desires should be tested by this statement, "Is this the Will of God for me?" With desire we build mental pictures of what we want, not what God wishes us to have. Desire pictures are the negative aspect of imagination. Our mental picture building must be under the absolute control of the Christ Consciousness. Then and only then will we build as God builds . . . perfectly. Every thought, dream, vision or mental picture must be the outpicturing of the Will of God in us.

Beloved, watch and pray, and keep free from the temptation to create according to your human desires. Keep your vision clear, high and holy. "I have also spoken by the prophets, and I have multiplied visions." (Hosea 12:10)

Peace be with you.

Questions on Daily Lesson Nineteen

1. *What have you been building into your consciousness?*
2. *Analyze the word Image.*
3. *How does man create?*
4. *What is the perfect way to create?*
5. *Explain the positive and negative aspect of Imagination.*
6. *How must desire be tested?*
7. *What must our mental picture building be controlled by?*

Verifying Visions

"Finally, brethren, whatsoever things are true, whatsoever things are honest, whatsoever things are just, whatsoever things are pure, whatsoever things are lovely, whatsoever things are of good report; if there be any virtue, and if there be any praise, think on these things." (Phil. 4:8-9)

What a wonderful way St. Paul has given us to differentiate between "visions" and "desires." What a glorious method to turn "desires" into "visions;" to sift the undesirable from the desirable! What a fulfilling way in which to recognize that the longings of our hearts can be the very yearnings of God which He wants brought into reality, for it is in our inner longings that our Lord speaks to us.

What thoughts come to mind for you to judge by the standards St. Paul puts forth? Let your fancy play. Would you like a new home or car? A better job? To express yourself creatively as a singer, perhaps? Or as an artist? Perhaps a writer? Would you like to find more joy in being a parent? Or husband? Or wife?

By now you are well acquainted with your chosen way to attune yourself with Creative Source, so become still; put on your protection; ground yourself; choose the angelic friends you would have with you. Be ready to adventure again in spiritual growth.

Of the many ideas which have crossed your mind, select one you particularly want to bring into evidence. This is a test pattern so content yourself with one project now. At another time you can work on all the others.

Be clear in your thinking . . . what have you chosen? . . . what do you really want? Write down your hope clearly, so that you can evaluate it for worthwhileness.

Begin now to check yourself with the criteria from St. Paul's letter to the Philippians: First, "Whatsoever things are true." Is the idea or thing you want true to your nature? An illustration to prove this comes from one of our sons. By the time he was three years old he showed a remarkable ability to work with his hands; to take things apart and put them back together again.

Soon we were getting old clocks from jewelry stores for him to work on, but by the time he was an adult, he chose to major in history in college, although continuing to be drawn to construction work during summer vacations. He taught school four years, but the mental, academic world frustrated him. It was not true to his nature.

He has since become a successful building contractor where he works with his hands as well as his mind. This is true to his nature. To pray for this would fulfill the first "whatsoever."

In judging the trueness of your own project, be specific but not covetous. Choose something you want because it is right for you, rather than the possession of another which you admire and want. God has given us enough talents and abilities of our own without impinging on those of another.

Will your aim fulfill your true needs?

If it is a different home, do you really need more room, for instance, or would the extra space sit idle?

If you are asking for a job with more authority, will you supervise wisely or do you want to express dominance?

When we ask if a dream can become a vision to be brought into reality, we are challenged to check our motives. If this dream is to become true, do you need to put more energy into your work, for instance? Should you learn more? Improve your personality? Learn to get along better with people?

For the dream to evidence, what do you need to slough off?

Write down your dream. Write down your abilities. Write down your deficits. Is your project true to your nature? Do you really want it? The choice is yours.

Take time to find out.

Become sure.

Believe.

When you are ready, work through the other "whatsoevers" using the same criteria.

"Whatsoever things are honest."

Do you really want what you are thinking about? Are you being honest with yourself?

Will you accept any responsibility which comes with the achievement?

Will you be at ease with the result?

Are you asking from pride or spite or greed or to get even?

Will your answer bring health, peace, prosperity, joy, love, fulfillment?

If so, your prayer is honest.

Evaluate your motives again.

Take all the time you need.

"Whatsoever things are just."

Have you fulfilled your part to bring about the results and the answer would therefore be just? Have you, for instance, worked well for a long time and deserve the better job? Then your prayer is just.

If you want to be a great singer, have you studied music ? Practised? Performed whenever possible?

Do you dream of being an artist? And have learned the basics of your craft? Followed your leadings as to sales markets and public contacts?

Are you prepared to work in a positive manner with your talent or your prosperity? Will you make the most of your new home?

Go over your background and intentions.

For a prayer to be "just" is to have laid a groundwork of effort, sacrifice and service . . . to have demonstrated a willingness to use the end product in an unselfish, useful way.

Prove to yourself that your prayer is just.

When you are satisfied, go on to "whatsoever things are pure."

Will your request let you "do unto others as you would have them do unto you?" (Luke 6:31) Are your motives untinged by possessiveness or pure personal gratification?

Would God be pleased?

Are you thinking of the good of all, or merely yourself?

What would you need to clarify in your actions and your mind to meet the question, "Is my longing pure?" Write down the good angles and those you need to get rid of and find the pureness so that you can get the fulfillment.

Take your time. You need not rush.

"Whatsoever things are lovely." Pray for beautiful

things as God would have much beauty in your life. There is beauty in all He has created.

If your desire is true, honest, just and pure, there must be beauty in it. Pray for more beauty, but beauty which expresses itself tenderly, gently, kindly; with understanding and trueness.

"Whatsoever things are of good report." If your longing has met the standards already set forth, expect answered prayers. Make a "good report." Speak in an outgoing manner, with expectation. Believe in what you have asked for. Your desires are becoming visions. Start claiming your answer both in your thinking mind and your speaking mind . . . not arrogantly, but quietly, confidently. You are meeting the requirements our Lord has set forth. You can affirm this.

No longer do you need to look at your lack and say, "I am poor," or "I am ill," or "I cannot express myself." Rather, from now on, say, "All my needs are met," or "I am well," or "I'm free to express myself," and it is so.

"If there be any virtue, and if there be any praise, think on these things."

As you have studied, you have planted the seed of Christ Consciousness within your heart. You have watered the seed with the Qualities of Christ and you have faith that it is growing and will blossom and produce fruit. You do not dig at the roots and check the growth and uproot the plant.

Just so with the vision you are producing. You will trust that the results are coming. If your dream is true, honest, just, pure, lovely and of good report, you have every right to expect a good fulfillment.

You are giving your request to God and trusting the Creative Force of your inner nature to bring it into fruition. You may be guided as to any changes which will or

96

VERIFYING VISIONS

will not take place in your life; your personality may be modified; new friends might enter your life.

Recognize all changes and give credit to God when your answers come.

In fact, give credit to God *before* the answers come. As St. Paul says, "if there be any praise, think on these things." Praise God for the vision you are going to have fulfilled. Thank Him. Acknowledge that of yourself you can do nothing, but that the Christ in you as one facet of God can bring anything to fulfillment if it is true, honest, just, pure, lovely; if you expect it and give thanks.

Can you already feel the dream enlarging within you and becoming a vision which is worth bringing into wholeness and sharing with others?

Good!

Conclude your quiet time, making sure you are well protected and grounded in God's entirety. Pray our Lord's Prayer, smile sweetly, yawn perhaps, and glory within yourself in a slow, delightful, expectant way.

The Christ Quality . . . Will

Beloved, this fruit of Will is one of the greatest lessons or tests that every follower of Christ has to meet. When we blend the human will with the divine, we have learned one of the principle lessons in this school of experience. Read carefully how our beloved Lord met this test. (Matt. 26:42) He leads the way, so let us follow Him.

THE STATEMENT

Thy Will is my will.

Luke 22:39–53

In Daily Lesson Two, a foundation stone called Faith was mentioned, but in the teachings of Christ we find a three-fold foundation . . . A trinity composed of Faith, Surrender and Service. Faith is the positive or right hand side of the triangle; Surrender or Will is the left hand or negative side. The base of the triangle represents Service which will be taken up later.

God has given man absolute freedom of choice on all planes of Being, physical, mental and spiritual. "Choose you this day whom ye will serve," (Josh. 24:15) is an unbreakable law. Freedom of choice is in the Inner Planes as well as the Outer. Angels, Masters of Wisdom and all others obey this law. Man must *will* to do the Will of God. Our beloved Lord came to teach us how to blend our human will with the divine. God's Will must be done on this earth as it is already done in heaven.

To understand Will better, let us think of it as two hands, right and left. The right hand represents the Will of God. It is positive and powerful. "Thy right hand, O Lord, is become glorious in power." (Ex. 15:6) The left hand represents the human will. It is negative and receptive. It is very necessary that we are receptive toward God and positive toward the world or outer conditions. However, very often the opposite is true. When the right hand and the left hand work together in order and harmony, then Good or God is manifested.

The Will is sometimes called, "the keeper of the gate." Remember, beloved, that it is the Will which is the rudder on your little ship of Personality in all experiences on all planes. You are the mate and must take your orders direct from the captain (God), if you would bring your ship into a safe harbor.

The lesson of Will is more submersion than submission. It is blending your human will with the divine until it becomes your greatest joy to do the Will of God. "For it is God which worketh in you, both to will and to do of His good pleasure." (Phil. 2:13) We must be willing to sink our personality, plans, hopes and fears, in fact our all, into the Will of God.

When we can say and mean, "Thy Will, not my will, be done," then we have mastered one of the most difficult lessons in the great school of earthly experience. Our joy will be fulfilled as we come alive, saying, "I delight to do Thy Will, O my God; Thy law is within my heart." (Ps. 40:8)

Peace be with you.

Questions on Daily Lesson Twenty

1. *Name the three-fold foundation.*
2. *Is freedom of choice on all planes of expression?*
3. *What does the right hand represent?*
4. *What does the left hand represent?*
5. *Name the keeper of the gate.*
6. *What is the difference between submersion and submission?*
7. *Name one of the most difficult lessons in the school of experience.*

The Christ Quality . . .
Law and Order

Beloved, this fruit is often overlooked by the seeking soul, but it is of the greatest importance that we express Law and Order in our spiritual experiences. Always remember that Law is active on all planes of Being, physical, mental and spiritual. Jesus Christ, our great example, recognized law. "Think not that I am come to destroy the law or the prophets. I am not come to destroy but to fulfill." (Matt. 5:17)

THE STATEMENT

I love Thy law.   *Matt. 5:21–48*

To realize that our God is a God of Law and Order, we need but to raise our eyes to the heavens above us. "When I consider thy heavens, the moon and the stars that Thou hast ordained." (Ps. 8:3) The Law and Order of our God is written above us in the movement of the stars and planets and in the unfolding and evolving life upon this earth. "Thou hast made heaven, the heaven of heavens, with all their hosts and the earth and all the things that are therein." (Neh. 9:6)

On the higher plane of consciousness, Law and Order rule undisturbed by the confusion of mankind. Unlike the laws of man, God's Laws are few and simple. The greatest is the "Royal Law of Love." "If ye fulfill the Royal Law according to the Scripture . . . Thou shalt love thy neighbor as thyself . . . ye do well." (James 2:8) Our Lord said the first and greatest commandment is love. Read Matt. 22:36–40. Jesus Christ came to this earth as the fulfillment of all law and He gave us Grace, which is another name for love; "that being justified by His Grace, we should be made heirs, according to the hope of eternal life." (Titus 3:7)

Beloved, to bring forth this Christ quality or fruit in your life, it is necessary to express Order to the best of your ability in your spiritual life. To read, pray and meditate part of the time, using your spiritual knowledge only when you are in trouble, will not bring forth an orderly spiritual growth. It is the daily communion with your Lord and learning to wait upon Him in every instance which brings forth Order. "I waited patiently for the Lord; and He inclined unto me, and heard my cry." (Ps. 40:1)

Do not always ask, but listen to what He has to reveal to you, His beloved one. "The Lord is good unto them that wait for Him, to the soul that seeketh Him." (Lam. 3:25)

The holy Lord Christ is not only your God but your teacher, friend and partner in the experiences of everyday life. He walked the hard road, the "Way of the Cross" to leave a clear path for your feet. And Jesus said, "If any man will come after me, let him deny himself, and take up his cross, and follow me." (Matt. 16:24)

Read in Luke 1:76–79 of the visit of the Dayspring to this earth. All the lesser laws are found within the great law of Love. When we keep the law of Love, we keep all the laws. Oh, beloved seeker of Light, only as you fill your own heart full of love toward all, do you find Light.

"Beloved, let us love one another, for Love is of God."
(1 John 4:7)

Peace be with you.

Questions on Daily Lesson Twenty One

1. *What is one of the most important lessons in life?*
2. *Where is God's Law written?*
3. *Name the greatest Law of God.*
4. *What is another name for Love?*
5. *Should you use your Truth only when in need?*
6. *Why is the "listening ear" important?*
7. *What is the "Way of the Cross?"*

The Blessings of Law

Our God is indeed a God of Law and Order. If we learn the spiritual laws and tap into them, Order will appear in our lives. This is Law and Order according to the highest Source. It cannot fail.

Sometimes we hear the statement that a person has broken one or more of the Ten Commandments. As with all of the laws of the universe, these Great Laws are inviolate. Rather than the laws being broken, we break ourselves on them. God's laws stand whole and perfect, unbreakable, unbendable, but always fair and loving and eternal.

Let Law and Order be as a promise to you . . . not a threat. Realize that to give thanks for the learning shown in the laws discovered and obeyed is to reap the benefits and joys of thanksgiving and obedience.

Pray the affirmative prayer of asserting that good is coming to you because you are doing your best and because of the Grace of God.

Give thanks that this is so.

As we have studied together we have established over and over that we must be willing for God to evidence His good answers to us. Check your willingness now. Are you still utterly committed for His goodness to come to you in His chosen way, rather than what you think would be best? Will you continue to name everything that happens to you as good, no matter if it does not seem to be? You must do this if you would build a path for God's beautiful answers to come to you.

Only as we are completely willing can we find goodness in every experience, whether or not it is tempestuous.

Check yourself in regard to some of the other laws we have learned:

Are you communing every day with your Creative Source?

Are you using the prayers of protection at least twice a day, preferably three times and even more often if you are in situations of stress?

Do you remember to "ground" yourself so that you are always in control of situations?

Are you becoming better acquainted with the Angelic Beings?

Do the many Christ Qualities come to your mind?

Do you expect them to blossom in the garden of your heart?

Is there joy in your studies?

Are your relationships with others improving?

Are you more friendly?

Do you respond more easily to people and situations?

Are you more prosperous? Contented?

These qualities which are unfolding in your life are the blessings you are getting.

Only you can know where you are.

Only you can show the evidence and results of your tuning into and obeying the divine laws which bring divine order.

Expect the good to continue as you go on with your learnings.

Give thanks that this is so.

Rejoice!

To do so, extend your hands, palms curved gently upward to form a cuplike shape.

Let our Lord pour blessings into your outstretched hands.

Absorb those blessings into the very core of you. Experience them; enjoy them; glow with gratitude.

Thus you are observing the laws of loving, listening and accepting.

As a result, the Law of Order fills you with God's good glory!

The Christ Quality . . .
Renunciation

Beloved, this is the fruit called Self-Denial. Do not avoid eating freely of this fruit for denial is a cleansing and eliminating process. We cannot refill until we are empty of self. All old conditions, thoughts, desires must give way to the new. We must forsake or renounce the old way of living so that we may come into the Christ Way.

THE STATEMENT

I will renounce all evil and hold to the good.
                                        2 Cor. 5:12–21

Beloved seeker, let us explain more fully the meaning of denial or renunciation. It is the mental self, not the physical self that is to be denied. The physical must be controlled and the emotional directed. Our Lord, Jesus Christ, warned us in Matt. 6:16–18, against the abuse of the physical body. This body we live in is God's holy temple. We must care for it as we would a shrine for "the Spirit of God dwelleth in you." (1 Cor. 3:16)

In the Bible the mental self is called, "the heart of man." "For out of the heart of men proceed evil thoughts." (Mark 7:21) Paul who understood the science of mind called it, "the carnal mind." "Because the carnal mind is enmity against God; for it is not subject to the law of God." (Rom. 8:7) It is easy to see that our Lord meant the denial of the mental self with its ambitions and selfishness. "If any man will come after Me, let him deny himself . . . " (Matt. 16:24) When we eat freely of this fruit of Renunciation, we cleanse our hearts, minds and bodies.

We must reject from our consciousness all self-seeking or carnal thoughts that the real self, the Christ in us, may come forth in all His glory. "To whom God would make known what is the riches of the glory of this mystery among the Gentiles; which is Christ in you, the hope of glory." (Col. 1:27) This work of elimination takes us back to the third daily lesson and the section entitled "Meeting Your Personal Christ." The same method that we used to remove the weeds from the garden of our hearts, we again use to eliminate negative thoughts from our consciousness for we become aware as time goes on that more and more old memories come to mind for healing and more and more actions present themselves as needing healing.

We must refuse to entertain in our minds all thoughts of hatred against any race or religious knowing. "There is no respect of persons with God." (Rom. 2:11) We must look upon all mankind as children of the one Father. "One God and Father of all, who is above all and through all and in you all." (Eph. 4:6) We must renounce all envious thoughts because we know, "The earth is the Lord's and the fullness thereof." (I Cor. 10:26) We must deny all condemning thoughts for we know that to judge another brings us into the same comdemnation. "Judge not that ye be not judged." (Matt. 7:1)

This, beloved, is substitution. It is not easy nor is it done quickly. The garden grows in beauty only with daily cultivation, so the garden of our heart requires daily care. We do not come into full consciousness of Christ at once. Day by day, like the flowers, we unfold in the sunshine of His love and presence.

"And the desert shall rejoice and blossom as the rose." (Isa. 35:1)

Peace be with you.

Questions on Daily Lesson Twenty Two

1. *What does denial do for us?*
2. *What self must be denied?*
3. *Give several names of this self.*
4. *Explain true renunciation.*
5. *Give four special points in this work of renouncing.*
6. *Can substitution be quickly done?*
7. *Do we come into a full consciousness of Christ at once?*

The Christt Quality . . . Zeal

Beloved, if you desire to know if you are bringing forth the fruit of Zeal in your life read carefully the questions given in this lesson. If your answers are more positive than negative, then that wonderful quality of the Christ . . . Zeal . . . is manifesting in you.

THE STATEMENT

I am zealous toward my God.

Isa. 59:16–21

As you climb the Mount of Attainment there are many resting places by the way, where you can stop a moment and review the past lessons and experiences. As you look back on your path you begin to question yourself.

First: Have I been faithful to Christ? In my tests on the lesson of Faith, have I remembered the three steps necessary to bring forth the flaming light of Faith? "The just shall live by faith." (Gal. 3:11)

Second: Am I "strong in the Lord?" Have I been loyal, courageous and patient with myself and with others? "The

Lord is the strength of my life . . . of whom shall I be afraid?" (Ps. 27:1)

Third: How wise am I? Is my wisdom from God or man? Do I lean on my own understanding? "They that seek the Lord understand all things." (Prov. 28:5)

Fourth: Am I loving? Do I use the great Trinity . . . . Love, Life and Light in my everyday life? "No man hath seen God at any time. If we love one another, God dwelleth in us, and His love is perfected in us." (1 John 4:12)

Fifth: What use am I making of the power God hath given me? Am I depending fully on the God-power within? "I can do all things through Christ which strengtheneth me." (Phil. 4:13)

Sixth: What am I thinking? Are my thoughts, dreams, visions and mental pictures becoming more Christlike daily? "Let this mind be in you which was also in Christ Jesus." (Phil. 2:5)

Seventh: Do I understand my Lord and His mission better? Am I more willing than ever to serve Him patiently and humbly? "Humble yourselves therefore under the mighty hand of God." (1 Peter 5:6)

Eighth: Is God's Will my will? Is it a joy to say, "Thy Will be done in me?" Am I willing to *let* God work through me? "Teach me to do Thy Will; for Thou are my God." (Ps. 143:10)

Ninth: Is my spiritual life in order? Am I neglecting my daily communion with my God? "Meditate on these things; give thyself wholly to them." (1 Tim. 4:15)

Tenth: Am I rejecting all that is not Christlike in my life? Am I daily removing the weeds from the garden of my heart? "Abstain from all appearance of evil." (1 Thes. 5:22)

Eleventh: What am I devoted to . . . the things of the Spirit or the things of the flesh? I cannot serve two masters. "No man can serve two masters . . . ye cannot serve God and Mammon." (Matt. 6:24)

Beloved, ask yourself these questions earnestly and prayerfully. No one has the right to ask you these questions. It is a sacred matter between you and your Lord. How much you are expressing the Christ quality of Zeal, only your Christ knows.

This quality manifests itself through a life devoted to Christ and Christ only, for Zeal is another name for devotion. "And they helped every one his neighbor and everyone said to his brother, 'Be of good courage.'" (Isa. 41:6)

Peace be with you.

QUESTIONS ON DAILY LESSON TWENTY THREE

1. *Explain the meaning of Zeal.*
2. *How do we strengthen our faith?*
3. *Illustrate the use of the Trinity of Love, Life and Light.*
4. *Explain the power of thought.*
5. *What is the Will of God?*
6. *What must we eliminate?*
7. *Give another name for Zeal.*

The Christ Quality . . . Life

Beloved, have your kept your daily appointment with the Lord Jesus Christ? Do you feel His consciousness flooding your Being like waves of golden light? Jesus Christ is both within and without. Within you as Love, Life and Light and without as the only manifestation of the Infinite that humanity can understand. "Who, being in the form of God, thought it not robbery to be equal with God." (Phil. 2:6)

These lessons are but sign posts along the Way of Attainment to point you to Christ. Read them often and study and pray that your inner eyes may be opened. "For now we see through a glass darkly, but then face to face." (1 Cor. 13:12)

THE STATEMENT

My life is hid in Christ.

John 6:44–58

We read in Rev. 22:2 that in the Holy City was the Tree of Life that bore twelve manner of fruit. We have called this fruit, "The Christ Qualities" and have eaten of it during the study of these lessons. This lesson on Life is most important because it is the second great principle in the Trinity of Love, Life and Light, or the Godhead. (See Daily Lesson Seventeen)

Love, Life and Light are but names for the Infinite One . . . the Almighty. "I am Alpha and Omega, the beginning and the ending, saith the Lord, which is, and which was, and which is to come, the Almighty." (Rev. 1:8) Beloved, the Lord Christ Himself is Love, Life and Light. All that we in our present state of unfoldment can comprehend of the Infinite One is in the Christ. "I am the resurrection and the life." (John 11:25)

Our beloved Lord Christ came to this world to give us Life. "I am come that they might have life." (John 10:10) Think constantly of the life in your body as the Christ life. All the manifestations of life in the outer world about it is the Christ Life, from the tiny seed to the distant planet. There is no death, no absence of Life anywhere. That which appears to be death is but a change of form. Life, like Love and Light, are eternal verities and Christ came to earth to reveal these truths to mankind.

Beloved, you are "children of the Light," climbing the Mountain of Attainment. On the summit is the beautiful Temple of Light with its three glistening steps.

The first step is called Christ Consciousness.

The second step is called Christ Qualities.

The third step is called Christ Revelation.

The third step is explained in the next four lessons. All these steps must be climbed slowly, patiently and prayerfully if we would enter the Temple.

"I am the Way, the Truth and the Life: no man cometh unto the Father but by me." (John 14:6)

Peace be with you.

QUESTIONS ON DAILY LESSON TWENTY FOUR

1. Name the Christ within.
2. Name the Christ without.
3. Where is the symbolic Temple of Light?
4. Who reveals the mysteries to us?
5. Is there absence of life anywhere?
6. What appears to be death?
7. Name the eternal truths and their Revealer.

Milestones Along the Way

The Christ Highway is concerned with the expression of the Love, Life and Light of the Christ Spirit in our lives in order to benefit both ourselves and others. Daily Lessons One through Twelve express the Love of the Christ as the birth of His Spirit within us.

The second group of twelve lessons expresses the Life . . . the growing qualities . . . of the Christ. In our studies we have allowed these to develop within us. We are expressing Life.

Just as the first twelve lessons were a complete unit to Mrs. Thedick, so were the second twelve. Again her little group financed the publication of a booklet, this time with twenty four lessons.

It was as "The Messenger" that these booklets were printed for this is the title given to Eleanore Thedick by the angels. She liked this title. She felt it explained the work she did since she faithfully shared the messages she received from the Heavenly Host.

Her human way of explaining her ability to listen, to hear and to share the guidance she received from inspired sources was simple. "The dear Lord looked around and found me and said, 'she will do because she doesn't know anything and has nothing to unlearn.'" In actuality, of course, she had learned life's lessons so thoroughly that all dross had been removed and she was a pure channel for God's truth to pour through.

She credited the prayers of protection, which she used faithfully, for a great deal of her ability to stay directly on her chosen path. Telling others of the power of these prayers was a great part of her work.

"You must remember," she would remind her students again and again, "the prayers of protection are a high vibration of energy which burn out after about eight hours. Less, if there is a crisis. The protection should be renewed in that time span or whenever there is an emotional or physical challenge.

"Don't feel threatened by this power," she would continue. "It isn't as though you are doing anything wrong if you don't protect. This is just a wonderful tool which will make your life easier if you use it."

Like everything else she taught, the decision to don the prayers of protection was left to the individual for she shared her wisdom rather than pushed a philosophy.

"All I know is what the dear Lord teaches me through His Word (the Bible) and through His helpers, the angels," she would say. "I'm glad to be a messenger for Him. It seems that I am to be faithful in keeping appointments for prayer, to listen and to share. You will have to find your own schedule and your own special dedication," she taught.

Every conversation seemed to contain these same characteristics. As she met a newcomer, two hands covered the one extended in greeting and her initial "how are you?" seemed to convey concern rather than perfunctory salutation. Even small talk was interjected with charming stories of her native England or family, but there was always a point which led to maturing of the mind or improvement of the body.

She was very much aware of current events, however, and kept abreast of the world news and politics through reading, TV and discussion. She applied her philosophy of life to political crises and social situations as well as personal difficulties.

During the Berkeley riots of the 60's, for instance, one of her students owned a college boarding house which was in danger of being sacked, not from personal spite, but simply because of its location in the area.

"Stay inside," she advised the young man. "Tune yourself into Universal Love. Pray that God's perfect plan shall come through. Do not waste vital energy on fear nor resentment, nor even sympathy. Give God *His* way. Trust completely that whatever is right will happen."

No rocks were thrown at the house. No windows broken. No fires started.

And this was good but this was not the ultimate aim nor expectation, you will remember. The aim was to tune into God's perfect pattern and to see it established. If the result had been other than lack of damage, it too should have been called good if the relinquishment had been total.

It would be her prayer that this book will point each of us toward that same goal.

The Temple of God

Beloved, the first four of the next twelve lessons symbolize the last step . . . the Christ Revelation. This step brings us to the "Temple of Light." At the door we meet the Supreme Master, our Lord Christ, and we sit at His feet and learn of Him. As we listen in the quiet of our own hearts, He fulfills His promise and reveals the holy mysteries of God to us. An understanding of these mysteries leads us to the Temple Courts.

These lessons only point the way, beloved seeker of Light. You must walk on the way, for to walk and talk with Christ is to become like Him.

THE STATEMENT

My body is God's holy temple.   *John 2:13-25*

In our first lesson we found our Lord addressing Nicodemus in symbolic language, but Nicodemus failed to understand Him. Symbology is the language of the Spirit and is constantly used in the Bible. This holy book is filled with hidden wisdom told in the form of symbols. It must be read and studied with the Spirit and not the letter. "For the letter killeth, but the Spirit giveth life." (II Cor. 3:6)

We learn in this lesson about our wonderful bodies, called temples in the symbolic language of the Bible. "Ye are the Temple of the living God." (Cor. 6:16) The two great essentials necessary to keep this temple beautiful is circulation of pure air and cleanliness within and without.

The circulation of air represents our thoughts. A small thought of hatred, resentment or criticism sent out to any one will pollute the air in our temples. We absorb that poison into our very being and the result is sickness. Beloved, you may have overcome hate, resentment and fault-finding, but still have your temple filled with fear and worry thoughts and a cleansing is necessary.

We must recognize the sacredness of our own bodies and strive to keep them "holy and acceptable" unto the Lord. This is the Way of Preparation for entrance into these Inner Plane Temples. There are temples of great beauty and magnificence in the Inner Planes of Being that are open to us according to our spiritual unfoldment.

We often enter them during our hours of sleep, but entrance is earned, not gotten through personal efforts. Do not *try* to enter through psychic power; rather earn entrance through soul unfoldment. Our bodies are the dwelling place of the Holy Spirit and we must permit this Spirit, or the Christ Consciousness, to flow unhindered through us. Our temple, then, becomes illumined with the glory Light of the Presence of the Almighty.

"Then shall the righteous shine forth as the sun in the kingdom of their Father." (Matt. 13:43)

Peace be with you.

QUESTIONS ON DAILY LESSON TWENTY FIVE

1. *Name the three steps to the Temple of Light.*
2. *What language is symbology?*
3. *What are our bodies called in the Bible?*
4. *Explain the effect in the body of negative thought.*
5. *What cleanses our Temple?*
6. *Should we try to enter the temples on the Inner Plane?*
7. *How can we illumine our Temple?*

Indwelling Your Temple

Each section of twelve lessons has given us the opportunity to become more sensitive to the teachings of our own indwelling Christ Spirit. In this third group of lessons we can know ourselves as being the Temple of God. We can experience ourselves as created in the Image and Likeness of God. We can express ourselves as God the Father; God as the Christ; and God as Holy Spirit while still living wholly in the earth experience. This is our opportunity to become attuned to God as Creator and God as human being.

This can be accomplished by making of yourself a five-pointed star with your feet on the ground and your head in the stars. Stand erect, feet apart, arms extended, shoulder high, palms up and hold your head erect. Feel the energy of the earth—the man part of you—rising through the feet to meet the tingling of the God part of you which overwhelms you from above. The top of your head is a receiving station for Creative Force. This is the very I AM center where the Christ Spirit from the universe can enter in and join with the Christ Spirit which is within you. Breathe deeply and let this very light of God enter you and go all through you, refreshing, healing, teaching you.

Your outstretched arms can be the meeting place for the earth forces from below and the heavenly energy from above to meet. They become one and you are perfectly attuned. Your hands are alive with healing energy. The force goes in through your left hand and out through your right hand. Use it for yourself if you have a painful need or send it to another simply by holding your right hand in an outward position and thinking where you would like your God-power sent. It will go where you choose to send it. Rejoice in the sharing.

Your feet are on the ground. Your head is in the stars. You are as you were meant to be, perfectly balanced. Luxuriate in this until the vital energy lessens and your arms slowly drop of their own volition to your sides.

You are the very Temple of the Living God.

Know this.

Show this.

Give thanks that it is so.

The Silence

In this lesson we learn of the Silence and the easy way to enter it. Jesus Christ spoke simply of the great Truths. As we unfold in consciousness and become more like Him, we also desire simplicity in all things.

THE STATEMENT

I am still before my God.   *Ps. 46:1-11*

Beloved, you hear a great deal about "entering the Silence." Many books have been written on this subject, yet there is much confusion of thought in regard to it. The Silence is but the name for the Inner Realm of Being which Jesus called, "the kingdom of heaven." He illustrated what this inner kingdom was like by many parables. This realm is both within and without. When we wish to bring forth results in the outer expression of life, we go within. This is but the fulfilling of a law. To create or bring forth anything, we must first think about it or "go within."

It is easy to enter the Silence if you take this simple way. After a while you can enter it at any time and any place, but in the beginning one has to follow certain rules until the subject is mastered.

Take a time when you are free from disturbance. Assume a restful position. If sitting, place the feet flat upon the floor, hands in the lap, palms upward.

Pray the prayers of protection. The importance of protective prayers cannot be too greatly stressed. Always use the prayer of the Wall of Fire or Flame (See Daily Lesson Ten) before entering the Silence. Beloved, you are a spiritual radio, constantly sending and receiving vibrations and messages. The Wall of Flame sets your dial, closing out the lesser vibrations or thought waves. Use also the powerful protective prayer, the Armour of God which St. Paul tells us about in Ephesians 6:11–17.

When we enter the Silence, we are seeking to tune in to the most powerful Source of all. It is the "station" called the kingdom of heaven. We choose to dial out all lesser stations which are broadcasting sickness, war, racial hatred or any other negative ideas. Our Lord said, "Ye cannot serve God and mammon." (Matt. 6:24) Therefore, to go into the Silence is to obliterate all but God thought and protecting ourselves with the Holy Name of Jesus Christ is the best way to do this.

It is next necessary that we build a place in our consciousness for the reception of our heavenly guest, Jesus Christ. It is the law of the mind to create an image, so to try to think of nothing will but open the mind to trivial and useless thoughts.

How do you see the Christ when your mind is still? A good way is to picture a white room with the holy Lord Christ standing in the center awaiting you. You can be utterly still before such an ideal and you will be in the Silence.

How easy it is now to speak to this Loving One. Tell Him all that is troubling you, "casting all your care upon Him; for He careth for you." (1 Peter 5:7)

As you do this, you feel a peace within your heart and you know that you have made perfect contact with that great spiritual broadcasting station, the kingdom of heaven.

Stay in the stillness, letting your thoughts merge with the thoughts of the Creator until there is an utter oneness, wordless interchange of energy and wholeness.

As you emerge from the Silence, remember to give thanks that you have been heard and answered, for "before they call, I will answer, and while they are yet speaking, I will hear." (Isa. 65:24)

Peace be with you.

QUESTIONS ON DAILY LESSON TWENTY SIX

1. *Give another name for the Silence.*
2. *Describe necessary steps to enter the Silence.*
3. *What is the most important point and why?*
4. *What does the Wall of Flame do for you?*
5. *Explain the Law of Mind.*
6. *What happens when you try to stop thinking?*
7. *Why should your mental picture be white?*

Silent Bliss

When one actually enters the Silence there is an inexplicable union between the Spirit of the Creator and the one who is created. It is a oneness in which words are unnecessary. Whether that bliss lasts but a moment or is there for a longer time, there seems to be no need for words of explanation or asking.

Nevertheless there are usually answers for the unspoken or the unasked when the time is over. The Oneness of the Creator contains all knowledge and all expression and all action, whether active or passive. The union itself transmits as much of that all-knowledge or all-expression or all-action as the human temple can hold in the time of togetherness.

There will be an understanding that everything we think, feel, know or do comes from our higher Source. Our time of contemplation can put us in tune with more and more of the divine resources which we express through the beauty and balance of our lives.

Be willing to spend time in the Silence.

Ask to spend time in the Silence.

Give thanks for time in the Silence.

Experience the Silence.

Learn from the Silence.

Share the good that comes from the Silence as you are guided by your God, not by your intellect.

Protect yourself before entering the Silence and upon leaving it.

Praise God that you have learned this way of communicating with your very Source in the Silence.

The Coin of Heaven . . . Service

INSTRUCTION TO THE SEEKER: DAILY LESSON TWENTY SEVEN

These lessons, beloved, are the orderly building of the Christ Consciousness in you. This is your "city four-square" mentioned in Rev. 21:16. This twenty-seventh lesson completes the third cycle of nine lessons each, in your study of the Indwelling Christ. Day by day as you practice His presence you will unfold the perfect pattern. "Be ye therefore perfect, even as your Father which is in heaven is perfect." (Matt. 5:48)

THE STATEMENT

Every day I serve my God joyously.　　　*Luke 6:17–49*

In our previous lessons, Service has often been mentioned, but not fully explained. In Daily Lesson Fifteen we find that the Christ Wisdom is symbolized by a temple. The seeker finds it necessary to pass through three gates before he can enter this temple. The names above these gates are Humility, Patience and Service. To receive of God, it is necessary to *give*. Service is the coin with which we pay our way along the path of Spiritual Unfoldment.

As we study the teachings of Jesus Christ, we find the mysterious Trinity appearing again and again. This time it is represented as Faith, Surrender and Service. Faith is the positive or right hand side of the triangle; Surrender is the negative or left hand side. The base of the triangle is Service, which is the coin of heaven. "With good will doing service, as to the Lord and not to men." (Eph. 7:7)

On this three-fold foundation rests the teachings of Christ. Hear His words, beloved, and understand, "If any man will come after me, let him deny himself, and take up his cross and follow me." (Matt. 16:24) When we follow Christ, it is necessary to deny the personality, have faith and surrender the human will to God and give joyous service.

Every service we do for another should be done as unto our God, looking only to Him for our reward. Let us rejoice in the privilege of service in the cause of Christ, no matter how humble or difficult that service may be. We must follow in the Master's footsteps, "who went about doing good." (Acts 10:38) We hallow and consecrate our daily tasks when we look upon them as temple service given freely to our God.

Our Lord told His disciples to, "lay up for yourselves treasures in heaven." (Matt. 6:20) What constitutes, "treasures in heaven"? Beloved seeker of Light, if you would have this treasure, these abundant riches of God, then serve freely in the Name of Christ. Service is the coin of heaven. "In the house of the righteous is much treasure." (Prov. 15:6)

Peace be with you.

QUESTIONS ON DAILY LESSON TWENTY SEVEN

1. *What cycle does this lesson complete?*
2. *Name the gates of the Temple of Wisdom.*
3. *What do Faith, Surrender and Service represent?*
4. *What self must be denied?*
5. *Explain, "Take your cross daily."*
6. *How can we consecrate our daily tasks?*
7. *What is the "coin of heaven?"*

Garments of Praise

Beloved, we have cleansed our temple. We have entered the Silence and presented our coin of heaven, so now let us clothe ourselves with the garments of Praise.

Later on we shall receive our new name, "The Overcomer." Then we shall be ready to enter the Temple of Light where we shall find the Masters of Wisdom and the Angel Hosts. Then we shall eat of the Bread of Life and drink the Living Water. "But whosoever drinketh of the water that I shall give him shall never thirst." (John 4:14)

THE STATEMENT

I will praise the Lord at all times.   *Isa. 61:1-11*

All through the Bible garments are mentioned, literally in Ex. 28:2, "and thou shalt make holy garments," and symbolically in Isa. 61:3, "The garments of Praise." As followers of Christ it is very necessary that we clothe ourselves in the "garments of Praise." What are these garments? Beloved, praise is but another name for thanksgiving or gratitude, sometimes called "rejoicing in

131

the Lord," in the Bible. When we lift our hearts to God in praise and thanksgiving for His countless blessings, we "cover" ourselves as with a garment.

This garment of Praise has the power to deliver and protect us. "They sang praises to God . . . the doors were opened, and everyone's bands were loosed." (Acts 16:25-26) If you wish delivery from any difficult condition, bless it and give thanks. Read Eph. 5:6-20. Before you rise from your bed in the morning, place this "garment of Praise" about you by joyfully giving thanks to your God for the new day and its new opportunities. "It is a good thing to give thanks unto the Lord." (Ps. 92:1)

Thanksgiving and gratitude are true spiritual foods and can be eaten freely. This garment of Praise is a robe, beloved, that anyone can wear, but to keep it from slipping off, it is necessary to fasten it with the "Jewel of Joy." "My mouth shall praise Thee with joyful lips." (Ps. 63:5)

One of the fruits of the Spirit is Joy. "The fruit of the Spirit is love, joy, peace, long-suffering, gentleness, goodness, faith, meekness, temperance: against such there is no law." (Gal. 5:22-23) This Joy is the jewel in the Christian's crown. Therefore be happy and be joyful. "I will greatly rejoice in the Lord. My soul shall be joyful in my God; for He hath clothed me in the garments of Salvation. He hath covered me with the robe of righteousness." (Isa. 61:10)

Peace be with you.

Questions on Daily Lesson Twenty Eight

1. *Name three things that must be done before we can receive our "robe."*
2. *What are the garments of Praise?*
3. *What power do these garments have?*
4. *Name two spiritual foods.*
5. *What jewel do we fasten our "robe" with?*
6. *Name one or more fruits of the Spirit.*
7. *In the Christian's crown, what jewel do we find?*

The Overcomer

Beloved, you are standing at the door of the Temple. You have fulfilled all the requirements demanded of a follower of Christ and a new name is now given unto you. It is one you have earned as you have come, step by step, along the Way of Spiritual Unfoldment.

THE STATEMENT

I am an Overcomer through Christ.   *Rev. 3:7–13*

The Path of Spiritual Unfoldment is symbolically an upward climb. Daily we overcome a selfish trait, a fear complex, a race thought or some private challenge. In this way we take one more step upward and onward, earning our new name, "the Overcomer." Our beloved Lord has promised the fruit of the Tree of Life to the Overcomers. "To him that overcometh will I give to eat of the tree of life." (Rev. 2:7) This fruit is the Christ Consciousness that you have been building daily within your own being. "that Christ may dwell in your hearts by faith." (Eph. 3:17)

To overcome anything means to conquer, subdue or master the thing or situation. An Overcomer is a lesser Master because he is taking the steps that lead to mastery by overcoming. The Overcomer is learning, but the Master knows and is now instructing others. There are great Masters of Wisdom manifesting on all planes of Being, some in their spiritual form and some in their natural bodies. Read 1 Cor. 15:40-44. They have overcome and now can manifest on all planes with ease. These are our Elder Brothers who, having reached Christ Consciousness, hold out helping hands to us. We seldom recognize these helping hands of Master Souls for they come to us along the natural channels of life. Their service, like the Ministering Angels, is impersonal and unselfish.

These great Masters never compel or control us, for a Master of the Right Hand Path always works with the Law and never interferes with free will. The help that these great souls give is through the channels of intuition and inspiration. Jesus Christ is the Supreme Master of all Masters and all teachers, helpers and Masters of the Right Hand Path serve humanity in His Name. As our Elder Brothers are Masters through Christ, so are we Overcomers through Christ.

"And he that overcometh shall inherit all things; and I will be his God, and he shall be My son." (Rev. 21:7)

Peace be with you.

Questions on Daily Lesson Twenty Nine

1 . What is our new name?
2. Explain the difference between the Overcomer and the Master.
3. Who are the Elder Brothers?
4. Why do we fail to recognize them?
5. How is their service given?
6. Through what channels do these great one give their help?
7. Name the Supreme Master.

The Realness of Being an Overcomer

Beloved, if anything in this book can become real to you, let the lesson of the Overcomer be that thing. Read and re-read this lesson. Know that the seed of the Christ Consciousness has grown within every part of you and you are ready for this new name.

You have taken the qualities of Faith, Strength, Wisdom, Understanding, Love, Power, Imagination, Will, Law and Order, Renunciation, Zeal and Life into yourself. You *are* the Temple of God.

You have experienced the Silence of union with your Creative Source; have been called to extend yourself to others as they will permit. You are filled with thanksgiving and with praise.

You have let the Christ Consciousness be within you, removing all which is unlike the perfections of your own divine plan. You have now been given a "white stone and a new name." (Rev. 2:17)

You are truly an Overcomer.

Savor this fact with all your five senses. Feel as though you can touch the substance and whiteness of the stone; let the words of your new name roll over the tasting organs of your mouth; breathe in the nuances implied; hear your name . . . an Overcomer . . . speak it aloud; see the words "a white stone" and "a new name" written in space as an accomplished fact!

Feel like an overcomer.

Act like an overcomer.

Give thanks that you are an overcomer.

Walk through life as an overcomer.

Through the Christ Spirit, you are confidently all new!

The Ministering Angels

Beloved, look up all the references to angels and their holy ministry of Service in the Bible. Pray for a new revelation and a clearer understanding of these messengers of God and their loving, unselfish service given down through the ages.

We are created a "little lower than the angels." (Heb. 2:7) The angels, however, are not to be worshipped for they are our brethren. "And I fell at his feet to worship him and he said unto me, 'See thou do it not: I am thy fellow servant and of thy brethren that have the testimony of Jesus,'" (Rev. 19:10)

THE STATEMENT

I give thanks for the protection of the angels of God.
Luke 1:26–38

The world does not recognize nor accept the truth of the angelic ministry, yet the Bible is full of incidents describing services the angels render to mankind. Their appearance and their work is found in the Bible from Genesis 3:24 to Revelation of John 22:16.

An angel announced to Mary that she would be the
mother of Jesus. (Luke 1:31) At the time of His birth the
angels sang joyously. (Luke 2:13–14) They comforted our
Lord during His trial (Matt. 4:11) and ministered unto
Him in His hour of greatest need. (Luke 22:43) He could
have called the Angel Legions to defend Him. (Matt. 26:53)
but had He done so, the scriptures would not have been
fulfilled. (Matt. 5:17) The angels rolled away the stone
from His tomb. (Matt. 28:2–3) They gave the words of hope
to a sorrowful world, "He is not here for He is risen as He
said." (Matt. 28:6)

After our Lord's mission on this earth was completed the
angels ministered to the disciples. (Acts 5:19–20) Beloved,
this angel ministry was not closed at the time our Lord
walked this earth. It is as real and potent now as then. The
help and protection of the angels is given to the children of
Light today as freely and as unselfishly as in the days of
long ago. "For He shall give His angels charge over thee, to
keep thee in all thy ways." (Ps. 91:11)

The word angel means messenger or envoy; one who car-
ries tidings or news. They are a race of intelligent Beings of
a higher order than man. "For Thou hast made him a little
lower than the angels." (Ps. 8:5)

Their office is to guard, direct, guide and carry out the
Will of God on earth and in the heavens. "Bless the Lord,
ye His angels, that excel in strength, that do His commandments, hearkening unto the voice of His word." (Ps.
103:20)

There are millions and millions of ministering angels ser-
ving the Godhead. (Heb. 12:22) Just as we find the powerful leaders of humanity upon this earth, so there are powerful angels of God leading their hosts to carry out the Will of
God. There are Angel Musicians (Rev. 8:6), Angel Singers
(Rev. 5:11), Children's Angels (Matt. 18:10), and Protecting Angels (Matt. 2:13).

All these you will find recorded in the Bible but there are many more in the Ministry of the Angels of which there is no written record. The usual appearance of the angels is described in Matt. 28:3, but if you wish to know how the leaders of the "Mighty Angels" look, then read Dan. 10:5-6 and Rev. 10:1. Beloved, a study of the Angels of God will bring a greater realization of the power and majesty of God to you.

"For He is Lord of Lords and King of Kings: and they that are with Him are called, and chosen and faithful." (Rev. 17:14)

Peace be with you.

Questions on Daily Lesson Thirty

1. *Who are the messengers of God?*
2. *Is the work of the angels well known on earth?*
3. *Name some of the work done by the angels for Christ.*
4. *Did the ministry of the angels cease with His resurrection?*
5. *What is the meaning of the word "angel?"*
6. *Are there leaders among angels?*
7. *What will a study of the angels reveal to you?*

Working with Angels

We are told in Daily Lesson Thirty that the Ministering Angels will work with and for us only if we invite them to do so. This could make the old adage that "fools rush in where angels fear to tread," a practical idea about which to think. It causes us to rue the many times we could have used help and neglected to request it, yes, but it may also make us stop and think of the many times we have impetuously tried to change the life of another to our ideas without being asked.

Are we learning from these lessons that God, like the angels, is instantly available but that even God does not push His will upon us? Is it becoming clear that we should invite . . . not beg . . . not harass . . . simply invite and then accept the help of God Almighty and His heavenly messengers, the angels, to enlighten us; advise us; comfort us; show us how to be joyful; useful; generous but not pushy; available but not overbearing?

Are we becoming aware of how we have gradually changed from the beginning of Daily Lesson One until we are now truly a new creation in Christ? Have we learned that we say "yes" or "no" to a more fulfilling, deepening life experience through realizing the broad spectrum which is our Christ, and responding as we feel He would have us do? There are no "maybe's" in the world of the Holy

Spirit. We either go with our perfect pattern laid out for us or we deviate. The choice is ours.

We are always free to choose: to say "yes" or "no" to the Light. The rules are inviolate. We follow them or we do not. Our chosen results follow. If we make the wrong decision, our loving God through the Christ Spirit and the Holy Spirit offers the gift of Grace and Forgiveness but will not push them upon us. The angels, also, are available to help.

Have you discovered a relationship with your own special angel . . . your guardian angel? Has the thought occurred to you, "if there are angels for some facets of life are there not angels for all areas of concern?" Have you decided to discover some of these by talking to angelic Beings, asking for more love, life, light, understanding, strength or friendship so that your whole life will be enriched?

If not, why not do so now?

What was the special seed you planted when you began your study? Speak the name aloud. In a firm voice claim that you have that quality. Invite the angels of that characteristic to be with you right now and to share with you and expect it to be so.

How would your angels communicate with you? There are as many ways as there are persons. An angelic experience is an individual meeting, just as each personal relationship is unique.

As you begin your adventure with your particular angel, ask as always that you be protected by the circle of Light which is so easily available. Feel yourself grounded firmly to the earth by allowing the security of the earth's magnetic pull to keep you from being too far out in your quiet time.

Remember that you are like a five-pointed star, firmly grounded, yet living in the heavens at the same time. You are beautiful and you are balanced.

Become still.

Spend a little time appreciating the new knowledge which has become part of you. Ideas will come into your mind and you will realize that each thought which comes is yours from God because you are attuned to Him and have shut out all that is not of His Source.

Quite simply now, address the particular angel by name with whom you would like to become better acquainted. It may be the Angel of Mercy, for instance. Or the Angel of Love; or Forgiveness; of Beauty and Balance; or Friendship; of Abundance perhaps, or Life.

Angels generally come in groups, so speak to the group by name, inviting the members to be with you. Ask questions if you like, as to how you may know they are there. Perhaps you will automatically accept their presence as you have become convinced of their readiness and willingness to be with you. You may actually sense a presence or even be given the gift of extra sensory seeing and the angel or angels will become visible to you.

An idea may come into your mind and this may be your angelic friend or friends. A personage may become real to you for a time when you have a great need.

Amazing things can happen when you let angels become a part of your life. One time we were driving on a busy bridge over a wide river and our right rear tire blew out. We tried but we couldn't find the directions for using the jack which came with the car. Suddenly two young men walked up to us and volunteered to help us. The tire was soon changed and they walked away. We never did know who they were nor where they came from for no car stopped near us.

Were these angels drawn to us by our need? We believe so. And we are still grateful.

The relationship you establish with angels can be rewarding to you and to them, no matter how it comes about. Angelic Beings are joyous when their services are used, just as we are pleased when we can share with another.

Your helpers are with you now. Communicate with them, verbally or mentally, remembering that the spoken word is even more powerful than the silent idea.

Say how you feel.

Share your joys.

Give them your woes.

Be still, then, long enough to be nurtured in a way which is acceptable to you. Experience the glory of release from the weight of your burdens.

Give thanks for your experience and express your appreciation to the angels who have been with you.

Renew the Christ Light around you.

Walk forth, knowing you are blessed.

The Living Water

Beloved, you have entered the Temple of Light, communed with the Masters of Wisdom and seen the vision of the Angel Hosts. In this lesson you learn of the Living Water promised us by Christ. "But whosoever drinketh of the water that I shall give him shall never thirst; but the water that I shall give him will be in him a well of water springing up into everlasting life." (John 4:14)

THE STATEMENT

Daily I drink the Living Water in the name of Jesus Christ.   *John 4:6–26*

In the first and last chapters of the Bible, water is mentioned, but the water mentioned in Rev. 22:1 is the Living Water or the Water of Life. Our Lord said to Nicodemus, "Except a man be born of water and of the Spirit, he cannot enter the kingdom of God." (John 3:5) Nicodemus confused the spirit with the letter and failed to understand this symbolic language. Water represents the great Mother Principle and Spirit is the Father Principle. To reenter the

146

kingdom of heaven, we must be reborn: "not in the flesh but in the Spirit." (Rom. 8:9) Water also represents a cleansing and purifying power.

This is very necessary in our lives before the quickening power of the Spirit can bring forth the new life. Beloved, many times we have had to go down into the deep waters of affliction and have said with the Psalmist, "The waters have overwhelmed us, the stream has gone over our soul." (Ps. 124:4) Pain and suffering are often blessings in disguise, coming to us over and over again to teach us sadly needed soul lessons. In this great school of life, we have the blessed opportunity of learning lessons and graduating from one grade to another. No person or condition can hold us back . . . nothing but ourselves.

As each experience comes to us, sometimes through the avenue of pain or grief, we must look carefully for the lesson which the experience has come to teach us. As we try to learn the lesson, we find something wonderful has taken place. This bitter cup we have been drinking is now filled with the pure, sweet water of Life and our lesson is learned.

Our beloved Lord knew when the cup of sorrow was at His lips that the lesson was submission of the human will to the divine. Hear His words, "Father, if Thou be willing, remove this cup from me; nevertheless not my will, but Thine, be done." (Luke 22:42) Beloved seeker of Light, look closely into every experience that comes to you for the hidden lesson contained therein. As "Overcomers" we must master lesson after lesson, drinking deeply of the Living Water. "Let him that is athirst come. And whosoever will, let him take of the water of life freely." (Rev. 22:17)

Peace be with you.

QUESTIONS ON DAILY LESSON THIRTY ONE

1. *What does water represent?*
2. *What has to be done before new life can come forth?*
3. *Name blessings in disguise.*
4. *Have we a special opportunity in the "school of life?"*
5. *Can anyone hold us back?*
6. *How can we find the hidden lesson?*
7. *What is the duty of the Overcomer?*

Life Is for Living

Life is for living! Our Lord did not tell us there would be no adversity, but He did promise us strength and courage to rise above our challenges.

Let us adventure together and discover this.

Become still through the techniques we have learned, taking time apart from our 'busy-ness'. We protect and ground our energies. We invite the Lord Christ and His angels to be with us.

We talk.

We listen.

We give thanks.

We can acknowledge and accept the help offered to us through the Forgiveness and Grace of God and our way will be easier. We can say "yes" to His plan for us and "no" to that which is inappropriate and we do this easily.

We dare to drink deeply of the Living Water of Life, thus finding value in our experiences.

We can know the special wonder which comes when we willingly and joyously submerge our personal will into the Divine Will, believing that God's Will is All-Good.

We can know the perfection of expressing that Divine

Will. When we do we have the rare privilege of appreciating each and every experience we have, whether it is easy or difficult.

We can thank God rather than question Him for to continually ask "why" or rehash experiences allows the sad side . . . the dark side . . . of life to have predominance.

Every time we waste vitality on remembering unhappiness, we give energy and strength to that emotion. We are not expressing faith. We are saying "no" to happiness rather than "yes," for we choose to be sad rather than happy.

Our studies have shown that we can choose to thank God for patience and have it, or we can choose the way of experience and learn our lesson.

The choice is ours.

The choice is always ours.

We can always choose to give thanks and enjoy the benefit of any of the Christ Qualities or learn the lessons through experience. The choice is ours. Either way we can follow The Christ Highway.

If we elect to give thanks and accept any characteristic or quality, we become alert, notice our reactions in any given situation, and recognize our growth. What are some of the situations for you where this can work?

In matters of employment, for instance, can you look beyond your present employer as the source of your abundance? Are you able to see that while the person or corporation through whom your pay check comes to you may be the channel for your financial security, he or it is not the Source? Are you willing to give thanks that, in spite of any apparently obvious appearance, you can depend on God for your supply when you trust that this is so? If so, this is letting your personal will be turned over to Divine Will.

When you are sick, do you recognize that illness is not the Will of God? Rather, it is the result of an intentional or unintentional misinterpretation of the laws of God. To give thanks for this knowledge is to tap into the Divine Will of God and open doors for healing to come through. The Forgiveness and Grace of God are contained in this as in any situation. How much more rewarding to look for and accept these attributes than to agonize by wasting energy to place blame on one's self . . . or another . . . or God.

Can you see the learning . . . the lesson . . . in every experience? To recognize the teaching; find the good . . . the value . . . is to tap into the Divine Will of God, leaving the personal will of man behind.

It is your joy to give thanks for the good in everything that happens. *Look* for good. *Experience* the joy of learning. *Enjoy* the good results which are yours.

To give thanks for every experience will truly add to the enlargment of your life. Your ability to enjoy and appreciate will be stretched and extended in a beneficial way.

Name every bit of Life to be Good . . . and it will be so!

The Bread of Life

In the Temple of Light is the Bread of Life and the Living Water, spiritual refreshment for the children of God. Beloved seeker of Light, drink deeply of this Water and freely of this Bread that your soul may be refreshed and strengthened. You eat and drink when you seek your God and express His indwelling consciousness in your daily life. "Thou shalt seek the Lord, thy God; thou shalt find Him, if thou seek Him with all thy heart and with all thy soul." (Deut. 4:29)

THE STATEMENT

I am fed with the Bread of Heaven.   *John 6:31–53*

Beloved, the spiritual part of your being is sustained and nourished only by the Bread and Water of Life. Jesus Christ said, "I am the living bread which came down from heaven," (John 6:51). Christ is also the Life of man. "For in him was life and the life was the light of men" (John 1:4), and there is no other way by which your soul can be fed. When you repeat the Lord's Prayer, do you realize that you

152

are asking for the Life of Christ, the bread sent down from heaven, to be given to you? To give anything, beloved, is to bestow, impart or transfer without a recompense. Therefore, unconsciously you are daily asking God to bestow Life, or the Living Bread upon you.

Our Lord tried to explain to the people gathered about Him that He had more to give than healing and food for their bodies. He tried to tell them that He had everlasting life to give them, if they would only believe or have faith. He was speaking of spiritual things but those who heard Him failed to understand. We also often make the same mistake because we interpret the spiritual according to our material ideas. Jesus was always teaching the spiritual truths to His disciples and the multitudes through symbology which is the language of the soul.

To the multitudes He spoke in parables, but to His disciples, He revealed the mysteries of the kingdom of God. Beloved, you are His disciple and He will reveal the mysteries to you as you eat the Bread and drink the Living Water.

No one can teach you as can this great Teacher of all time. Books and teachers are good only for a while. There comes a time when you enter the Holy of Holies within the Temple. There you meet the great Teacher face to face and then you are able to say with Thomas, "My Lord and my God." (John 20:28)

"For the bread of God is He which cometh down from heaven and giveth life unto the world." (John 6:33)

Peace be with you.

QUESTIONS ON DAILY LESSON THIRTY TWO

1. *Explain spiritual eating and drinking.*
2. *Why did Jesus say He was the Living Bread?*
3. *What does the Lord's Prayer give us?*
4. *How did Jesus teach the multitude?*
5. *How did Jesus teach His disciples?*
6. *Who will reveal the mysteries to you?*
7. *Who do you find in the Holy of Holies?*

The Tabernacle

Beloved, in the temple you find many wonderful mysteries. You meet the great Masters of Wisdom and the Angels of God and you drink the Living Water and eat the Bread from Heaven. In this lesson you learn of the three departments of the Temple or Tabernacle. "Loose thy shoe from off thy foot (understanding); for the place whereon thou standeth is holy." (Joshua 5:15)

THE STATEMENT

Today I enter the secret place of the most high.
Ps. 20:1-9

In Ex. 25:9, we read of a certain divine plan revealed to Moses regarding a tabernacle. Note that three important places are mentioned in it: first, the Tabernacle or Outer Court; second, the Holy Place or Inner Court; third, the Holy of Holies or the Secret Place of the Most High.

Now let us take the symbolic side of the description of the furnishings in the tabernacle. There are three special places, but all are needed to bring forth the perfect plan. The Outer Court symbolizes the body of man, "know ye not that ye are the temple of God?" (1 Cor. 3:16) Also this Outer Court represents the many who are seeking their

155

God. They pray and study earnestly preparing for that day when the Christ within calls and they enter the Holy Place.

Another name for this Holy Place is "The Sanctuary." The seekers for Light know it as the "Great Within," and our beloved Lord spoke of it as the "Kingdom of Heaven." Three symbols are found in the Holy Place, the shewbread, the golden candlestick and the altar of incense. In our spiritual studies we find bread symbolizes the life of Christ given freely to mankind. "I am the living bread which came down from heaven." (John 6:51)

The golden candlestick with its seven lamps kept constantly burning by the attending priests represents the golden glory Light of Christ. Seven is a period of peace and rest so necessary when entering the Holy Place.

The altar of incense symbolizes our earnest prayers rising constantly to our Creator. "Let my prayer be set forth before thee as incense." (Ps. 141:2)

In the Jewish Tabernacle, the Holy of Holies was unlighted and separated from the Holy Place by a veil. No one was permitted to enter except the High Priest and he entered but once a year. In this Holy of Holies was the Ark of the Covenant. In this Ark were the Tablets of Stone on which was written the Laws given to Moses. The word ark means a receptacle and this shows us plainly that the Word of God or His Law, is within us. "And this shall be the covenant . . . I will put my law in their inward parts and write it in their hearts." (Jer. 31:33)

The Holy of Holies is the Sacred Place of the Most High within us. It needs no candle, "for the Lamb is the Light thereof," (Rev. 21:23) and Christ, the Lord, has removed the veil for us that we may enter. Then "we all with open face beholding as in a glass the glory of the Lord, are changed into the same image, from glory to glory, even by the Spirit of the Lord." (2 Cor. 3:18)

Peace be with you.

QUESTIONS ON DAILY LESSON THIRTY THREE

1. *Name the three departments in the Temple.*
2. *What does the Outer Court symbolize?*
3. *Give three names for the Holy Place.*
4. *What is the symbology of the shewbread?*
5. *Explain the symbology of the golden candlestick.*
6. *Explain the symbology of the altar of incense.*
7. *Describe the Holy of Holies.*

The Glory of God

Beloved, it is very necessary that we unfold gradually into a consciousness of this indwelling Christ. If the veil were lifted suddenly we could not, in our present understanding, bear the unveiled glory of God.

We may desire with all our hearts for more illumination and a deeper revelation of the Mysteries. We may feel that our unfoldment is painfully slow, but we are building for eternity. Haste in spiritual unfoldment is fatal to the attainment of the end which is the Christ Consciousness.

THE STATEMENT

Lift up your heads, Oh ye gates, that the King of Glory may come in.   *Ps. 24:1-10*

It is very interesting to read in the Bible about the glory of God. In Heb. 12:29, we read, "Our God is a consuming fire." This fire is the divine flame. It is in the heart of every one of God's children, burning away the dross that the gold may be purified. It is the flaming Light of Christ in humanity and the creative urge in the heart of nature.

158

David wrote in Psalm 19:1, "The heavens declare the glory of God."

There are many records of this divine flame becoming visible. Moses had to veil his face when he came down from the mountain and Jesus was transfigured before His disciples. "His face did shine as the sun and His raiment was white as light." (Matt. 17:2) Read Ezekiel's vision of the glory of God. (Ezek. 1:26–28)

Beloved, you are walking the path of Soul Unfoldment, hand in hand with your teacher and friend, Jesus Christ, and His light is within you. This divine flame is the glory of God and will shine more and more through you as you try to live the Christ Life daily. As you can do this, your very presence will comfort and bless all those whom you meet in your journey of life.

Let this inner radiance of the Christ Love, Life and Light shine forth in you. Feel its warm glow in every part of your being and then radiate it forth to bless all God's beloved children everywhere. This is the law, beloved.

First, make your contact with your own indwelling Lord Christ and become conscious of this divine flame of Love, Life and Light within you. Realize your oneness with Him who is, "the mighty God, the everlasting Father and the Prince of Peace." (Isa. 9:6) Now, beloved seeker of Light, send forth this Christ Consciousness to all the world over the spiritual radio in His own blessed Name.

"Arise, shine: for thy Light is come, and the glory of the Lord is risen upon thee." (Isa. 60:1)

Peace be with you.

Questions on Daily Lesson Thirty Four

1. *What is the glory of God called in the Bible?*
2. *Why did Moses have to veil his face?*
3. *How did the prophets describe the appearance of this glory?*
4. *What must you do to let this flame shine through you?*
5. *What effect will it have on others?*
6. *Explain the law of this inner radiance.*
7. *What is the spiritual radio?*

The Supreme Master

Beloved seeker of Light, do not let the call of the outer world, "Lo here, lo there is Christ," (Mark 13:21) dull your inner ear. To find Christ we must look within ourselves first. "For in Him we live and move and have our being." (Acts 17:28) Having found our Christ within, we then look without and see Him in nature and in the face of our fellow man. As we grow in spiritual consciousness we hear His voice, "that still small voice," (1 Kings 19:12) with our inner ear. We see him with our spiritual eyes, He who is "the author and finisher of our faith." (Heb. 12:2)

THE STATEMENT

I acknowledge Jesus Christ as my Master and my Lord.
Col. 1:9–27

When our beloved Lord walked this earth, He taught that through humility and service one entered the kingdom of heaven. In Matt. 23:10, we read, "neither be ye called Masters for one is your Master, even Christ." He knew that those who followed Him were Overcomers, not

Masters. The Overcomer is striving for perfection, but the Master has it.

Jesus Christ also knew who He was. He rarely revealed it, but we read in John 13:13, "Ye call me Master and Lord: ye say well, for so I am." The mystery of the Holy Trinity or the Godhead, our Lord touched on but lightly in His teachings. He spoke of three, the Father, the Son and the Comforter or the Holy Spirit. Even His closest friends failed to understand that He spoke of the Father within, and not of a Being without, for they said, "show us the Father." (John 14:8-9)

The Lord Christ was the complete manifestation of the Father, "for in Him dwelleth all the fullness of the Godhead bodily." (Col. 2:9) In John 14:26 we read of the promised Comforter or the Holy Spirit which is the consciousness of Christ and which will bring all things to our remembrance.

In the Gospel of John, Jesus is called, "the Word." "In the beginning was the Word and the Word was with God." (John 1:1) We read of this Word again in Rev. 19:11-16. Take these Bible quotations and meditate upon them. Jesus Christ told us plainly that the way to the Father was through Him. "I am the Way, the Truth, and the Life: no man cometh unto the Father but by Me." (John 14:6)

Perhaps to some, the idea of Christ in Form may seem too limited. They like to think of Christ as Spirit, Substance, Cosmic Energy, the Absolute. He is all that, and more than we in our present state of unfoldment can comprehend. How can the children of men understand love unless it is clothed with a body and expressed in a form? How can we understand Life unless it is expressed in the outer as well as the inner and clothed in the myriad forms about us? It is necessary that wisdom, courage, creative ability and energy be expressed before we can understand them. We live in a world where the formless or the unseen is constantly manifesting in form or in the seen.

"All things were made by Him; and without Him was not anything made that was made." (John 1:3)

Peace be with you.

QUESTIONS ON DAILY LESSON THIRTY FIVE

1. *Where must we look first for Christ?*
2. *How do we enter the kingdom?*
3. *Did Jesus know His real identity?*
4. *Name the Three that Jesus Spoke of.*
5. *What is Jesus called in the Gospel of St. John?*
6. *Why must Love be expressed in a form?*
7. *Can we understand Love, Wisdom and Energy better when we see them in form?*

The Supreme Master

This is the last lesson and the cycle is closed in your study of the indwelling Christ. Your "city foursquare" is now completed. You have been given the perfect pattern. As you practice His presence daily, you unfold like the flowers and become a living rose in the garden of the King.

THE STATEMENT

I will dwell in the house of the Lord forever.

Rev. 21:1-17

Beloved, the study of the greatest mystery of the ages is God in man and man in God, but the Word had to become flesh before we could understand. "and the Word was made flesh, and dwelt among us, and we beheld His glory." (John 1:14) An abstract ideal will remain in the visionary state unless made concrete or given some kind of a form or body. In 1 Cor. 2:8 we read of the Lord of Glory and how He took the form of men "and took upon Him the form of a servant, and was made in the likeness of men." (Phil. 2:7) Paul wrote a letter to the Philippians and in it the mission and nature of Christ was made very clear. Read it in Phil. 2:5–11.

Jesus Christ, our Lord, brought Love, Life and Light to a world sadly in need. He, the Supreme Master of all Masters, was willing to make the greatest sacrifice of all, and confine the glory and majesty of the Godhead within a human body. "For unto you is born this day in the city of David, a saviour, which is Christ the Lord." (Luke 2:11)

Beloved seeker of Light, Jesus Christ, the Lord, has walked and talked with you during the study of these lessons. He has instructed you so that His Consciousness may come forth in you. These are His words of Love to you. Read them often. Meditate upon them, "that ye would walk worthy of God who hath called you unto His kingdom and glory." (1 Thess. 2:12)

Child of Mine: Behold, I stand at the door of your heart and knock and I call to you. My call is the call of Love which knows no boundary or limitation. The very love you feel in your heart is My Love within you. Recognize all love as My Love, the Love of Christ.

My call is the Call of Life. I came into the outer world to teach you how to live. The life beating and throbbing within you is My Life. Recognize every expression of Life as My Life, the Life of Christ.

My call is the Call of Light. All Wisdom, all illumination and inspiration come from Light. I, the Christ, am the Light of the world. Acknowledge Me and I will lead you into Light.

Beloved One, you have the divine right of choice. Free will is granted to you upon this earth and in the highest heavens. I cannot make your choice for you; but the more you choose Me as Lord Christ, visible and invisible, formless and form, giver and gift, the more you become like Me.

I have called down the Ages through the prophets, teachers and writings and I have spoken through the lips of the inspired ones. Today I call to you, My beloved One, "Come unto Me, that you may have Love, Life and Light." "My Peace I give unto you. My Peace I leave with you." (John 14:27)

"It is done. I am Alpha and Omega, the beginning and the end. I will give unto him that is athirst of the fountain of the water of life freely. He that overcometh shall inherit all things; and I will be his God and he shall be My son." (Rev. 21:6-7)

Peace be with you.

QUESTIONS ON DAILY LESSON THIRTY SIX

1. What is the "city foursquare"?
2. How do you practice the Presence?
3. What is the greatest mystery of the Ages?
4. Why was it necessary for the Word to become flesh?
5. How can abstract ideas be made concrete?
6. What special gifts did Christ bring to this world?
7. What was His greatest sacrifice?

Go Forth and Serve

Beloved Seeker of Light:

You have now completed this course. Your knowledge of the Christ is greater than ever before. You are well along on your own Christ Highway.

If it please you, gather two or three other Seekers of Light around you. Have a definite study period with them. The Lord Christ can use you to heal and help others since it is by giving that we receive.

The lessons learned will help you through all of your life situations. They are impersonal and universal, touching all who follow Jesus Christ.

Share your appreciation with our Lord as you savor this prayer-poem:

Beloved Lord Christ:

> We drink at the fountain of Thy Love
>   and we become loving and forgiving.
>
> We drink at the fountain of Thy Life
>   and we grow strong and unafraid.
>
> We drink at the fountain of Thy Wisdom
>   and we find Thy freeing truth.

The Infinite Spirit of all Love enfolds us.
The Infinite Spirit of all Life strengthens us.
The Infinite Spirit of all Light illumines us
     and we walk joyously and thankfully in the
     Light of our indwelling Christ.

                              Amen.